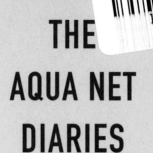

THE
AQUA NET
DIARIES

—

Big Hair, Big Dreams,
Small Town

THE
AQUA NET
DIARIES

Big Hair, Big Dreams,
Small Town

JENNIFER NIVEN

GALLERY BOOKS

New York   London   Toronto   Sydney

Photo credits: pp. 1, 9, 159, 206 © WayNet.org; pp. 17, 102, 144, 152, 226 courtesy of
Jeff Shirazi; pp. 22, 41 courtesy of Jack F. McJunkin Jr.; pp. 29, 36, 45, 108, 183, 255,
264 courtesy of the Richmond High School *Pierian*; pp. 46, 58, 70, 114, 131 courtesy of
Penelope Niven; pp. 53, 91, 94, 120, 167, 277 courtesy of the author; p. 81 courtesy of
Beth Jennings-White; p. 127 courtesy of Laura Lonigro; pp. 137, 174, 235, 293 (left), 295
(left), 299, 303, 305, 307 courtesy of Pyle Photography; p. 194 reprinted with permission
from the *Palladium-Item*, Richmond, Ind.; pp. 215, 238 courtesy of Aldo Lonigro; p. 248
courtesy of Olan Mills Portrait Studio; p. 272 courtesy of Rebecca Scheele; pp. 290–91
courtesy of Wahlberg Panoramic Photography; p. 293 (right) courtesy of Stephen
Hunton; p. 295 (right) courtesy of Steve Kunken; pp. 297, 301 courtesy of David Geier
Photography; p. 309 courtesy of John Hreno III

G

Gallery Books
A Division of Simon & Schuster, Inc.
1230 Avenue of the Americas
New York, NY 10020

First Gallery trade paperback edition February 2010

GALLERY and colophon are trademarks of Simon & Schuster, Inc.

For information about special discounts for bulk purchases, please contact Simon & Schuster
Special Sales at 1-866-506-1949 or business@simonandschuster.com.

The Simon & Schuster Speakers Bureau can bring authors to your live event. For more
information or to book an event, contact the Simon & Schuster Speakers Bureau at 1-866-
248-3049 or visit our website at www.simonspeakers.com.

Designed by Nancy Singer, Class of 1979
Illustrated by Alexandra Davis Ivey, Class of 2012

Manufactured in the United States of America

10 9 8 7 6 5 4 3 2 1

Library of Congress Cataloging-in-Publication Data

Niven, Jennifer.
  The aqua net diaries : big hair, big dreams, small town / Jennifer Niven.
     p. cm.
  1. Richmond High School (Richmond, Ind.)—History. 2. Niven, Jennifer—Childhood
and youth. 3. High school students—Indiana—Richmond—Social life and customs.
I. Title.
LD7501.R462N48 2009
373.772'63—dc22   2009017453
[B]

ISBN 978-1-4169-5429-3
ISBN 978-1-4169-5920-5 (eBook)

for Joey—
best friend forever

In so many ways,
the story couldn't have been
written without you

And for Richmond, Indiana,
my hometown

American girl,

American boy,

Living in a small town.

Dreaming of the great big world

And all that lies beyond . . .

— *"Back Again in Richmond,"*
original song by
Jennifer McJunkin & Joey Kraemer

Contents

I keep everything, and that includes every high school note I ever wrote and every note that was ever written to me (and believe me, there were *a lot* of them). If I quote a note in this book, it's an actual note from high school written during a class when I was supposed to be paying attention. I have also kept every partially written journal, every notebook, every high school drama program, sports ticket, photo, school paper, newspaper, story, poem, play, song (or any other type of creative anything I may have written), and every audiotape I ever made. Keeping these things was something I did with the intention of helping out my biographers one day, back in Indiana with my big dreams about becoming an Oscar-winning actress, international rock star, and Pulitzer Prize–winning writer. Little did I know how useful they would be to me when writing my own story.

Many of the names here are real. Some have been changed. Everything that happened is true as I remember it.

Richmond High School

High School Is (Almost) the Same Everywhere

Special times and special places
Special friends together;
The moments pass so quickly,
But the memories last forever.

> —*Motto, Richmond High School,*
>   *class of 1986*

If you had found me in 1986, walking down the halls of Richmond High School in Richmond, Indiana, and said to me, "One day, someone will pay you to write a book about your years going to school here, and people will actually want to read it once it comes out," I would have said, "I'm sorry, I think you have me mixed up with someone who lives in a much bigger and more interesting place. There is absolutely nothing to write about except how much I can't wait for high school to be over." Then I would have laughed and laughed and written notes to all my very best friends (during class, of course) saying, *Can you believe this? People are crazy!*

The very thing that distinguished my high school experience to me back then was that it was undistinguishable. To my teenage mind, it was dull, interminable, and I couldn't wait for it to be over. It wasn't that I didn't have fun or friends or enjoy myself, I just didn't see anything exceptional about it while I was living it. Not like my mother's experience—she was the one with the stories. She grew up in a charming town the size of a postage stamp in North Carolina, which was already more charming than Indiana because everybody had accents. Everyone knew everyone else and, yes, they were bored, too, but they made their own fun. In addition, she grew up in the 1950s—a decade with style and glamour. I grew up in the 1980s. We listened to Prince and Madonna and to hair bands. Our own hair was enormous. We wore parachute pants and Peter Pan boots and Swatches all the way up our arms. There was nothing charming about it.

My best friend Joe Kraemer (whom I met in tenth grade) was invited to a Halloween party a couple of years ago where the theme was Come as Your Worst Nightmare. He thought of every scary monster through the history of time, before concluding that his actual worst nightmare was himself in high school, right down to the big hair and oversized glasses and desperate need to fit in.

So this book came about by accident. It was never something I intended to write. If anything, I only wanted to leave high school far, far behind me—forever.

• • •

The idea for the book came about when I traveled to Russia in 2005. It was there I met Anya, who was sixteen. She was living in the tiny village of Novoye Chaplino, which is nestled along the eastern coast of Siberia. The village is populated by three hundred Siberian Yupik and a small number of Slavic Russians and Chukchi. Chaplino was once a thriving little whaling village with a whale processing factory, which now sits in ruins. Whale bones littered the ground, which was dotted here and there by wildflowers. Sled dogs wandered the dirt streets of the village, scavenging for food. Chaplino is void of trees and surrounded by Tkachen Bay—part of Senyavin Strait—and soaring mountains. The only road comes from the neighboring village of Providenia. Every few months, someone arrives by boat or by ship, as we did—aboard an icebreaker with Quark Expeditions. Otherwise the people of Chaplino are cut off from the world.

There is a school in the middle of the village that also serves as the town gathering place. The villagers invited us there for a show, and offered us whale blubber and hot tea as we sat on bleachers and watched schoolchildren, ages six through eighteen, perform traditional dances and athletic demonstrations. Anya was one of the best dancers.

Afterward, I asked her about what it was like to grow up in Chaplino. As far as I could see, you could not find a place more different from Richmond, Indiana, with its farms and tractors and Trans Ams and mullets and food festivals and sports, sports, sports all the time.

"It is sometimes so quiet," Anya said, and she laughed. "Here we are all in one school, even the young ones. A lot is expected. I wish sometimes there were new boys because we know the old ones so well." As she talked, she glanced now and then at a tall boy in a blue hooded shirt. He had black hair and was one of the athletic performers. "There is nothing to do, and we are bored in class. I am good at dancing but I am terrible at English. I do not like math." She laughed again. "It is hard sometimes to feel good about yourself because others"—she nodded at three girls standing across the gym—"like to say things behind your back. This is not fair, but there is nothing you can do to keep them from talking. I dream of going to Moscow one day after graduation. I think it might be better there."

Anya wanted to know what high school was like in America. "It must be very different," she said.

I thought before I answered her that, for me, high school was dating Eric Lundquist and Alex Delaney, flirting with Tommy Wissel, and wishing Dean Waldemar had asked me out. It was parties at Teresa Ripperger's and Eric Ruger's, and feeling snubbed by the cheerleaders. It was hating algebra and geometry and all things math, competing in speech meets, and wanting desperately to get excused from P.E. It was spending the weekends with my best friend Joey and with my other friends, trying to think of something fun or interesting to do. It was dreaming of the day I would graduate and be released from my school and my town.

"Actually," I said to Anya, "I think high school is really much the same everywhere."

When I returned to the States, I thought, *I'll write a fat comprehensive book on high school—on its history and its origins.* I started researching and writing, and all the research and writing put me to sleep. I fell right over onto my laptop. To keep myself awake, I decided to illustrate some of the history with funny stories from my own high school experience—crazy little adventures that I'd had, that my friends and I had lived through. What came out on the page were stories of a simpler time and place—funny, poignant, silly tales about a girl who never felt quite at home (but wanted to) in the enormous lone high school in her small Indiana town, about a rare friendship, about an eventual loss of innocence, and about some very big dreams. And this, not the dry and boring history book, was the story I ultimately found myself wanting to tell.

When I told my classmates what I was doing, they said, "Seriously? And someone is *paying you?*" And they began to laugh, just like I would have if I had been them.

I said, "Yes, and I want you to be characters."

They quickly stopped laughing. "With our real names?"

"Yes."

"What stories will you be including?"

"Only the interesting ones," I said, which made them wonder if I should use their real names after all (eventually—remarkably—many of them decided it was okay).

The most extraordinary thing about this journey is that I realized my mom isn't the only one with a charming story to tell. The more I wrote—and wrote and wrote—the more I realized what a special time high school was for me, too. I went to high school in America's heartland, in a pre-9/11 world. Nothing bad had happened to me yet. Everyone I'd ever known was still alive and happy. My parents were still married, although I didn't know yet that they were on the brink of separation. Life was innocent, good. There was angst, but it mostly involved having a bad hair day, finding the next party, worrying about saying and doing the right thing, wrestling with geometric theorems, trying not to die of boredom, and wanting to be noticed by the one boy we all loved more than anything. It was a time when we were fearless and invincible, when all our firsts were still ahead of us—first time behind the wheel of a car, first date, first love, first heartbreak, first drink, first job, first vote, first time leaving home to go out into the great big world. It was a time when anything was possible.

This is the story of one girl's high school experience. Some of it is universal and some of it belongs just to me, but in it, I hope you will find some of your own experiences, and some of yourself—the self you were then, the self you've become.

Orientation

During a record-breaking heat wave, RHS students obediently ended their summer vacations and wended their way back to stuffy classrooms and halls, almost ready to start another year of listening, studying, learning, and socializing. For some of us, it was our first time ever at the high school, and that in itself was terrifying but exciting. There was so much ahead of us, and we could feel it in the air. What would happen to us there? We were about to discover why they call these the best years of our lives.

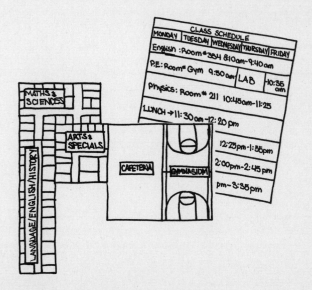

Downtown Richmond;
Richmond on a map;
one of Richmond's
many festivals

America's Main Street

Indiana . . . is a garden
Where seeds of peace have grown,
Where each tree, and vine, and flower
Has a beauty . . . all its own.

—Arthur Franklin Mapes, "Indiana" (state poem)

When I was growing up, there were 36,000 people living in Richmond, Indiana—a fact I always found
astonishing because, for me, the town consisted of: my parents; my neighborhood playmates; and the people I went
to school with, namely my best friend Joey; my next best

friends (a constantly revolving group); any boy I happened to be dating at the time; the popular crowd (of which I was a sometime member); and Tom Dehner, the boy we all admired. My Richmond felt much smaller than 36,000 people. In fact, I wondered where the rest of them were.

We moved to Richmond from Maryland in 1977, when I was entering the fourth grade. When my mother told her mother—also born and raised in a tiny North Carolina town—that we were moving to Indiana, Grandmama said, "Why on earth do you want to do a thing like that? Nobody moves to Indiana."

I had to agree with her. At first sight, I thought Indiana was the ugliest place I had ever seen. "Just remember," my mother told me, "what is ugly to you is beautiful to some people." As we crossed the state line from Ohio into Indiana, I looked out the window of our white Ford Pinto at cornfield after cornfield. At one point, there was an actual tractor driving down the road. A tractor! And I thought how wrong my mother was. I couldn't imagine anyone thinking Indiana was beautiful.

Our first week there, we experienced our first tornado. Clouds gathered and the sky turned green over the roof of the house we were renting until we could find one to buy (maybe this would change my parents' minds, I thought, praying for the tornado to come and not kill us but maybe do enough damage to scare them into leaving). There was wind and rain and the sky got greener and greener and I thought God Himself was probably showing his own displeasure at my parents' decision to move us to the Midwest. My mom and I, and our two cats and dog, buried ourselves under blankets and pillows while my dad slept right through it and never even woke up.

The next day we emerged from the storm just fine, without any damage to the house or our car or ourselves. My father was even well rested. But the cats had had all they could stand. Princess and her sister Michael (named for Michael Jackson, one of my first true loves) managed to unlatch a screen in a second-floor window and set themselves free. Together they set off down the Great National Road—the nation's first highway, otherwise known as America's Main Street—past Earlham College, past Cox's Grocery, past Miller's Milk House and the gun store, racing east toward freedom and home until my father, by some miracle, chased them down and brought them back.

Before I even unpacked, the first thing I did after we moved into our new house at 720 Hidden Valley Drive was to sit on the green-carpeted floor of my new bedroom and write a story. I illustrated it myself with pictures of a moving truck and cornfields and a girl with long brown hair and a sad face. It was called "My Life in Indiana: I Will Never Be Happy Again." After I finished, I took it downstairs to my parents and handed it to them. I didn't say anything, just placed it in my mother's hands, waited till she and my dad had read the title page, and then turned around and left the room.

In Hoosier City everything was a dark gray. The mail boxes were gray, the people's clothes were gray, what they ate was gray, and the sky was gray. Not one person was happy.

To my nine-year-old mind, moving to Richmond was a torture akin only to, say, moving to Mars. The local newspaper was filled with alarming stories: *Man Bites Tree. A man received two 180-day suspended sentences for* *bark off trees and breaking Christmas lights with* *the city's courthouse square.* And: *Piglets Are Boar* to Be w. .d. *A 270-pound wild hog wandered the area north of KOA Campground sowing its seed before being shot to death by local farmer Jerry Fairchild.* That article appeared on the front page, just below the headline: *Woman Decorates House for Christmas with Dryer Lint.*

The Richmond we knew was one of area festivals—in addition to the Rose Festival, there was the Pioneer Days Festival; the Hay, Hoosier Neighbor Festival; the Beef Festival (where they crowned an actual Beef Queen); and, in neighboring Preble County, the Pork Festival (which, in addition to a Pork Queen, featured a Hummel Figurine Look-alike contest and a Porkettes Microwave Demonstration). A local dance group, the Senior Steppers (ages sixty-four to eighty-two), performed medleys of armed forces songs, country, and Christmas tunes regularly at each of these.

Every year in Preble County, there was a Make It with Lard Contest, in which local ladies competed to make actual sculptures out of lard. In nearby Franklin County, there was a Bake It with Lard Contest. And for the yearly Rose Festival, Richmond's own Joy Ann Cake Shop proudly created the World's Largest Cookie, and Wick's Pies of Winchester baked the World's Largest Apple Pie (topped by 300 gallons of vanilla ice cream by Wayne Dairy). Every Fourth of July there were fireworks at Glen Miller Park (not named for the bandleader), which one of the three local radio stations broadcast over the radio. They called it "Fireworks for Shut-Ins" and this is how it went: "There goes a blue one!" "There goes a red one!"

These were things that clearly did not happen anywhere

else, especially not in Maryland, where people sailed in regattas and attended flower shows and, generally, behaved themselves with dignity.

At Westview Elementary School, my new Richmond classmates talked of two things—gymnastics (the girls) and basketball/baseball/football (the boys)—as if these were the only interests anyone could possibly have. During summers, most of the girls attended cheerleading camp, where they put their gymnastics training to good use, while the boys went to camps of their own—basketball, baseball, football. In gym class, we were graded on our ability to work the balance beam, the parallel bars, and the pommel horse. I hated the balance beam because I had a fear of heights. I never learned to cartwheel because I didn't like to be upside down. Most girls could do cartwheels on top of the balance beam.

In Maryland, I knew exactly who I was and what my place was in the world. I had played tennis and piano. I had danced and painted, and written stories about prisons and the Vietnam War. I planned to be a rock star or an archaeologist or an astronaut or an actress or a writer or a private detective when I grew up. I didn't play team sports and I wasn't a cheerleader, and so, I was completely unprepared for Richmond High School.

There are 109 classrooms in the high school and the main building measures 695,422 square feet—the equivalent of twelve football fields. This square footage does not include two gymnasiums, the cafeteria, the library, the counselors' areas, the art museum, the automotive shop, two day-care centers, the auditoriums, swimming pool, indoor and outdoor tracks, tennis courts, football stadium, or the Tiernan Center, the gymnasium that opened the winter of my junior year.

Indiana is home to nine of the ten largest high school gyms in the country. When it opened, the Tiernan Center was the largest and was featured in *Sports Illustrated*. The old gym, Civic Hall, only sat something like 4,000 people, which, for Indiana, was considered downright shameful. The Tiernan Center seats 8,100. It has indoor track facilities, a weight training room, two indoor tennis courts, six basketball courts, and twelve volleyball courts. In addition to being the high school gym, it is the town's largest gathering place.

My senior year, Richmond was named an All-American City by the National Civic League. The official town sign—the one that greeted visitors with *Richmond, Indiana—the Rose City, Home of the Rose Festival and Hill's Roses*—was taken down and repainted so that *All-American City* could be added to it.

I was the All-American girl living in the All-American City. But from the moment we moved to Richmond, I knew I would get out one day and go someplace bigger and faster, someplace where wild hogs didn't roam the streets and where men didn't eat the bark off trees. During my high school years, I was a member of the orchestra and the speech team and a history team that competed in a national championship. I wrote for the school paper and edited the literary magazine. The boys liked me, but a lot of the girls were mean. I was never the Homecoming Queen.

Yet even though I knew that I was only passing through, that I was on my way to Somewhere Else, I still desperately wanted all the things anyone wants: to be popular, to go to all the cool parties, to fit in. And while I was there, living in that world—in Richmond, in that enormous high school on the hill—I wanted to be just as much a part of it as anyone.

Student Life
Part One

WELCOME TO RICHMOND HIGH SCHOOL.
An education is very important today—more important than ever. Your experience can be fun, but no one is promising that it will not involve hard work. Our expectations are high and we want you to give your best effort to make your experience and our experience worthwhile. Do your homework each day for each class. Use the library/media center—it is yours. Ask your parents and teachers for help with your assignments. Prepare yourself for the best! I hope you have a good experience at Richmond High School.

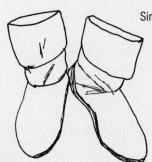

Sincerely,
Denney G. French,
Principal, 1983–1984

Rob Jarrett

Cheerleaders

Cheerleaders must be full of enthusiasm and school spirit at all times. They are in charge of coming up with ideas to keep the student body fired up. Cheerleaders perform as a team so they must follow team rules. Cheerleaders should be neat and attractive. They must be loud so they can be heard.

> — *RHS cheerleader requirements*

The summer before high school, I walked the mile through my neighborhood to Hook's Drugstore, which sat in a strip mall on the Great National Road just outside Hidden Valley, where we lived. Hidden Valley was one of the nicer neighborhoods in Richmond. Not as fancy as Reeveston, which was where all the rich people lived, but fancier than most. It was where the people who worked at

Earlham College—"liberals" like my parents—raised their families.

I walked up to Hook's every day to buy *Charlie's Angels* trading cards, Bonne Bell lip gloss, and, most of all, to see Rob Jarrett, who worked at the cash register. Rob Jarrett went to Test Junior High School and lived on the other side of town, but his dad owned all the Hook's drugstores in Richmond. He made Rob work at one of them every summer so that he could learn responsibility.

Rob Jarrett was the prettiest boy I'd ever seen close up. He looked just like Rob Lowe, with brown feathered hair and a white, white smile. He was so gorgeous that I would have hung his poster on my wall, if there'd been one—right next to Rick Springfield and John Taylor from Duran Duran. We had been flirting for weeks.

One day he asked me to meet him after work. We sat outside Hook's drinking sodas, and tried to get to know each other.

"Are you excited about high school?" Rob Jarrett asked.

"I guess."

Our high school was terrifying. It sprawled in all directions, from one end of Red Devil Boulevard to the other. It seemed miles long and just as wide. There were 2,500 students and you only got five minutes to go from one class to another.

"Are you excited about high school?" I asked.

"I guess. They had a good team last year."

Rob Jarrett had been playing football since eighth grade. He was planning to try out for the junior varsity team at RHS.

"So what did you do in junior high?" he asked.

"Oh, you know," I said, "hung out with friends. Things like that."

"No, what other kinds of things. Like, were you a cheer-leader?"

"No," I said. Cheerleaders were silly. I was better than that. I was comanager of the boys' football team with my friend Heather Craig. We washed uniforms and got to be in the school picture with the team. I had even dated a couple of the players—Darren Lawler and Brian Yoder, who was cute until he turned mean.

"Oh." He sounded disappointed.

"I was in the Travel Club," I said. We had met only a couple of times and mostly just looked at the atlas and talked about faraway places like Egypt and Greece.

"Really?" His voice was flat, distant.

"And the orchestra."

He looked down at his drink. I hoped he wouldn't think I was an orchestra geek or a band fag, which was what we called the kids who lived for band. These were the ones who never wore anything but school colors and were always car-rying their instrument cases with them, no matter where they went. I was only in the orchestra because I played the cello, but my life didn't revolve around being good at it. The fact was, I would rather have played electric guitar, but when they were handing out instruments in the fifth grade, that wasn't an option, and I'd been assigned the cello because I was tall. "And the Drama Club," I said. I did like to act. I had been writing, producing, and starring in my own plays—like Blindness Strikes Mary, my version of the true-life story of Mary Ingalls, Laura's blind sister, which I had written in fourth grade, as well as the antismoking play my cousin Ashley and I had written and performed one sum-mer for our grandmother (a passionate smoker)—since I was little.

Rob Jarrett yawned, covering his mouth with tanned knuckles. He wore a Band-Aid on the little finger. It made him seem rugged.

"And choir," I said. I loved to sing, although I wasn't very good at it. Still, I had managed to make choir every year.

Rob Jarrett just sat there.

"I was president of the speech team." I thought about all the medals I had won.

I considered the history team I had been a part of with four other students. We had taken it upon ourselves to create the team during after-school hours and had won first prize in the state history contest two years in a row, once for our oral history of our junior high school, the first junior high school in the country, the other for a skit on the Underground Railroad. I decided not to mention this.

We sat, not speaking. Everything was very still. The heat came up off the pavement and made the air ripple. Rob Jarrett's interest was drifting. His shoulders had slumped a bit. He played with the tab on his soda can. He stared across the parking lot, past the Big Blue Store, where they sold tires and toys and farm equipment and where my dad had once taken me to meet Burt Ward, who played Robin on the TV show *Batman*. Rob Jarrett looked off toward Dairy Queen and his brown eyes were sad. I was losing him.

"I was a pom-pom girl in the eighth grade," I said.

He turned to me and his whole face got bright, like someone had pointed a flashlight at it. "Really?"

"Yes. We marched in a parade and everything."

I didn't tell him that I'd *had* to be a pom-pom girl, that any girl in the orchestra with an instrument too big to carry—in my case, the cello—was forced to be one in the 1981 St. Patrick's Day parade when we marched with the newly formed band that would represent Dennis Junior High School. He smiled his white-toothed megawatt Rob Lowe smile. "You want to go to Dairy Queen?" he asked. He stood up, the sun catching the golden lights in his brown feathered hair. He held out a tanned, Band-Aided hand to me.

"Yes," I said, taking it.

Walking over to the Dairy Queen, I knew I'd just learned my first lesson about high school: boys love cheerleaders.

Jennifer on her beloved tricycle

Driver's Ed

So I forgot which way is right,
So the stoplight was out of my sight,
So I missed the four-way stop,
So I made the forty-foot drop,
So I ran over the yellow curb,
So I lost the wheel and began to swerve . . .

— *"Driver's Education," original song by Jennifer McJunkin*

The summer before high school began, I was eligible to take Driver's Education. The Driver's Ed students came from the four corners of town, from four different junior high schools, converging in the middle of Richmond at the gigantic school on the hill. Each of the junior highs had a distinct personality: Hibberd, in the run-down area of town, was home to the black kids and the hoodlums of all races, or "hoods," as we called them; Pleasant View, situated on the edge of town, out by the hospital and true farm country, was home to the farm kids; on the bucolic west side of town, close to Earlham College, was Dennis, where all the "liberal" Earlham kids, including me, went to school; on the comparatively bustling east side of town, out by the mall and the restaurants, was Test, which was filled with the rich, upwardly mobile, power-hungry kids, some of them descendants of Richmond's original forty-seven millionaires.

Most everyone who attended Test lived in a neighborhood called Reeveston. This was the closest thing Richmond had to Beverly Hills. Reeveston was grand and tree-lined, dotted with an eclectic mixture of stately homes—brick Victorian, Georgian Revival, Colonial Revival, English Manor.

It was a well-known fact that if you came from Test, you were, but for the rare exception, guaranteed popularity and success in high school. This was because privilege and money mattered, even in high school and even in a factory and farm town like Richmond.

We would have orientation in August, when we would walk around the school and get our student handbooks and be given our locker assignments and meet our teachers. But Driver's Ed was the first time that kids from Hibberd, Pleasant View, Dennis, and Test were all brought together.

The first day of Driver's Ed, I could spot the kids from Test, because they were the ones who seemed cool and collected and completely at ease. There was a confidence to them that came from money, from having known their place in the town, in the world, since childhood.

The rest of us were a different breed altogether. We chattered nervously and dropped our pencils. Some kids smelled like cigarettes. One boy had dirt under his finger-nails. Another had acne so bad that he looked as though he had a nasty case of chicken pox. There was one girl so enor-mous that she had to sit in the very back of the classroom on a bench. There was a girl named Martha Schunk who dressed in sweater sets and looked forty. She raised her hand repeatedly and told on people. Our teacher, Mr. Kemper, had unnaturally black hair that shone blue in the light like crow feathers, and he wore button-down shirts with short sleeves and a tie. He was the kind of man who had prob-ably been, once upon a time two or three hundred years ago when he was our age, good-looking.

In the classroom, we studied the Driver's Education Man-ual and practiced driving on simulators. With the lights out, we sat at individual computer screens, with steering wheels, a brake pedal, a gas pedal, and a gearshift. On the screen, little computer-generated people would fling themselves into the middle of the road or drivers from other cars would throw their doors open suddenly or animals would wander into the street. It was my favorite part of class. At the steer-ing wheel, I was Kelly Garrett (Jaclyn Smith), my favor-ite Charlie's Angel, driving my beige Mustang. I expertly dodged the errant pedestrians, deer, and runaway shopping carts while tailing the bad guy and looking glamorous.

Some of the boys, like Tommy Wissel, turned the simula-tors into a video game. Tommy had gone to Catholic school through the eighth grade, and after that he went to Dennis, where he quickly earned the reputation as a fun-loving trou-blemaker. He brought with him an air of mystery because Catholic school seemed exotic and foreign. We knew that instead of teachers there were nuns, and that, in addition to classes, students were required to go to mass. Tommy regaled us with stories of dropping Pop Rocks into the holy water at mass so that they fizzed like firecrackers throughout the service. His life's ambition was to be the laziest professional athlete ever.

During simulators, Tommy ran over every computer-generated pedestrian and curb on purpose, and then talked back to our teacher, Mr. Kemper, when he told Tommy to stop it.

"You can't pass Driver's Ed if you don't pass simulators, Mr. Wissel," Mr. Kemper said. Mr. Kemper never called us by our first names. For some reason, it was always "Mr. Wissel" or "Miss McJunkin." We found it maddening.

"So?" Tommy said. "I'll just take it again next summer."

Tommy had lots of cousins, and there was always someone to drive him places, and besides, Tommy was the sort who didn't think twice about driving illegally. The Wissels were famously wayward. They were all manfully handsome and loved to fight and have fun. Everyone said they got their high spirits from their mother and their temper from their daddy. Roughhousing was in the Wissel blood. It was why many of them didn't have all their front teeth—they were always getting them knocked out in brawls.

"Fine," Mr. Kemper said, because he knew he couldn't win. Mr. Kemper was one of those teachers, like so many I had known, who seemed resigned to his fate. He always looked as if he was kind of surprised at the path life had chosen for him, but as if he didn't have the energy or the strength to change it. He ultimately gave Tommy a D in simulators, which meant that Tommy passed Driver's Ed and Mr. Kemper never had to have him in class again.

When my classmates and I weren't actively engaged in simulators, we were busy checking one another out. Tentative friendships were already forming. After years of knowing the same old people, here, suddenly, were all these new ones. It was like a curtain being lifted to reveal a brand-new world.

The Test kids fascinated me most. They were shiny and golden—as much as anyone in Richmond could be—as if they came from somewhere else. Their king was Tom Mangas, who had reportedly been president of the student council. He was tall and blond with long, tennis player legs, blue eyes, and a big nose, the kind that immediately brought to mind Jimmy Durante or Telly Savalas. He wasn't great-looking, but he had so much confidence that you thought he was. He was smart and clever and funny and he loved to argue with teachers, like Mr. Kemper, who was no match for Tom intellectually.

"Who can tell me the proper procedure for exiting a parallel parking space?" Mr. Kemper asked. He sat behind his desk, hands folded.

"Put the car in reverse and pray to Jesus," said Tommy Wissel.

"That's enough, Mr. Wissel," said Mr. Kemper. Tom Mangas raised his hand and Mr. Kemper looked at once hopeful and wary. "Mr. Mangas?"

"I need some more information before I can answer the question," Tom said. "For instance, how far am I from the curb and from the cars in front of me and in back of me? Am I on a hill or on flat ground? Am I on a busy street or on a residential street or in an alleyway? Am I surrounded by cars at all, because if not that simplifies things."

Mr. Kemper covered his face with his hands and began rubbing his temples.

I thought Tom Mangas was the most exciting boy I had ever met, and every day during class, we made eye contact.

We eventually reached the part in the course where we'd had enough practice on simulators and were let out on the road, three to a car, with one of several teachers sitting shotgun, feet hovering over the passenger-side brake. I had Mr. Fleagle, who normally taught Health and P.E. and looked just like a weasel. He was tall and skinny and his eyes were too close to his nose. He always looked as if he had just popped up out of the ground and was having trouble seeing in the sunlight, or like he was smelling something unpleasant.

I was the only girl in my car, which meant I spent most of the time flirting—with Tommy Wissel and Mike Shockney, *not* with Mr. Fleagle. I wasn't a bad driver. The only thing I couldn't do well was parallel park.

One sunny afternoon when it was my turn at the wheel I accelerated a little too hard when backing up. We jumped over the asphalt and into a cornfield—Tommy yelling: "Yeah! Floor it!"—and Mr. Fleagle slammed his foot against the emergency brake on the passenger side of the car so that we came to a really hard stop and almost went through the windshield. He shouted, "For God's sake, McJunkin! Brakes! Brakes!" He couldn't stand girls anyway, especially behind the wheel of a car. He thought they should all be taking home economics, learning the things that would be useful to them later in life, like cooking and sewing. I know this because he said these very words to me while we were sitting in the cornfield.

Then he made me get out of the car and sit in the passenger's seat. He got behind the wheel and, after checking each mirror at least five times, slowly backed us out of the corn. "Dude, that was awesome," Tommy said to me.

The next morning, Mr. Fleagle came to class and handed Tommy the keys. "I want you to get on the interstate and just drive," he told him. Mike Shockney and I sat in the backseat while Tommy drove up and down I-70 going as fast as he damn well pleased. Up in the front beside him, Mr. Fleagle closed his eyes and took a nap.

Back in the classroom, Mr. Kemper began showing us films. Each day, he showed us one gory film after another about every possible horrifying thing that could happen to us in a car. The most horrific of all was one about underriding, which was what happened when a car followed a semi-trailer truck too closely and then accidentally crashed into its rear end and went underneath it. Nine times out of ten, this led to decapitation, but sometimes—rarely—people survived, usually living out the rest of their lives as vegetables.

As we sat there in the dark watching accident film after accident film, eyes huge, the color drained from our faces, even Tom Mangas and Tommy Wissel fell silent, except for a "Great Jesus" or a "Holy shit" from Tommy every now and then. At night, when I slept at all, I dreamed about people getting their heads chopped off.

On the last day of class, Mr. Kemper perched on the end of his desk and told us we were, for the most part, a good group of kids and that we'd all passed.

"Of course, it doesn't much matter," he said. "It will be a miracle if any of you live to be twenty-one."

Somehow I got an A– in Driver's Ed. And on the last day of class, Tom Mangas asked me to a movie. I decided I was ready for high school. I might never drive again, but clearly the boys I would meet there would be so much more exciting than the ones I had known at Dennis.

Jennifer and Joey

Best Friends

My best friends are Heather, Beth, Maya, Tia, Regina, Tina, Rhonda, Vicki, Sharonda, Becky, Andrea, Susie, Shannon, Kara, and Ned. My other best friends are Kelley, Melissa, Merri, Julie, Nancy, Shelley, Maida, and the paper boy who lives near us. His name is Matt Hanes and he is 15 years old and he hits Maya and I on the head with the paper.

— *Jennifer McJunkin, "My Life in Indiana," September 25, 1977*

On the first day of Geometry class, first period of my first semester, Bernie Foos called me to the board to draw a trapezoid. I stood there, chalk in hand, and had no idea what to do. I drew a sort of fat, drunken triangle and then sat down. Mr. Foos crossed his arms and gave a fifteen-minute lecture on the basics of geometry. "How can we hope to learn when we don't even know our triangles?" he said.

A boy sitting next to me leaned over and said, "I hate all things math." He wore glasses and had hair more shiny-blond than Marcia Brady.

I said, "Yes."

When the bell rang, the blond boy and I walked out of class together. He said, "My name's Joe Kraemer. You may not know this, but we're going to be best friends."

I said, "Oh, really?"

He said, "Yes. In fact, I think we're already best friends. Call me tonight and I'll prove it to you."

He gave me his number. I called him that night and we talked for four hours. It was then I learned: He loved to write, just like I did. He was trapped in Richmond, just like I was. He was counting the days till he could leave. He felt above the place and beyond it and like he wasn't really a part of it, yet he wanted badly to be a part of it, like I did. He was from Richmond, but he wasn't *of* it. It was platonic love at first sight.

One month later, he broke into Mr. Foos's room during lunch and changed one of my grades and three of his own and also two grades of Alex Delaney, the cutest boy in the class.

"Joey!" I said, after he told me about it. "What if you get caught? What if Mr. Foos finds out?"

"No one will ever know." He was unnervingly calm.

I let the enormity of what he'd done roll around me and over me and through me. Then I said, "Why did you only change one of mine?"

"Because you were doing better than me. I needed more help."

We went to class the next day and watched Mr. Foos carefully. I didn't breathe as he pulled out the grade book and took attendance, running his finger down the page.

Mr. Foos ran his finger all the way down to the end of the list and then closed the book and put it back in the desk. I started breathing again as he got up and walked to the board and began to draw a perfect triangle.

One weekend, not long afterward, Joey picked me up in his mom's red Oldsmobile Calais, and we barreled down I-70 East from Richmond to Dayton, Ohio, at ninety miles an hour, singing "Rebel Yell" at the tops of our lungs. This was our very favorite song to drive to Dayton to. I balanced pictures of Tom Dehner on my knee. I had stolen the pictures from the school paper, where I was a staff member. Joey craned his neck to see. "Hold them up," he said. "So I can get a better look."

"This one's my favorite," I said. In it Tom and Pierre Hogg were wearing their football uniforms. Tom's fist was raised in a cheer.

"Oh, that's a good one," Joey said. "Let me see that."

"He looks so good here," I said.

"Yes," said Joey.

We both sighed.

All of a sudden, the car lurched and went careening toward the median. We looked at each other and then down at the dashboard.

"What was that?" I shouted over the music.

"I have no idea," Joey shouted back.

We kept singing and driving, and after another mile, the car started thumping and bumping in a way we didn't recognize.

I turned down the music. We listened. The car thumped and bumped. "I think we have a flat tire," I said.

We were, of course, in the far left lane, the fast lane. We

looked over our shoulders and no one was coming because there was never any traffic on the I-70. Joey steered the car in the direction of the far right shoulder. The Calais drifted and wobbled in slow motion, finally limping to rest safely off the highway.

We sat there in silence. "Now what?" Joey said.

"Do you have a spare tire?"

"I don't know." For about five minutes, Joey searched for a way to pop the trunk. After he found it, he got out of the car and went to check. I waited. He came back. "No spare."

"Do you have a jack?"

"Hold on."

He disappeared and then reappeared a minute later. "No jack." He got back in the car and we sat there. "Now what?"

We looked around us. There was only highway as far as the eye could see. I suddenly felt very small and very sixteen.

"We have to get help," I said.

We locked the car and climbed down the gulley, then up the hill beside it. At the top of the hill was a wire fence and across the fence was a neighborhood of small brown tract houses, each exactly the same as the one next to it. Joey held the fence wires apart so that I could slip through, careful not to pull my hair or clothes. Then I held the wires for him. We began walking through the neighborhood.

Joey stopped in front of a house. "This is as good as any," he said. He marched up to the front door and rang the bell. No answer. We went to the next house and rang the bell. No answer. We tried the next house. No answer. By the time we reached the last house on the block, we were in a panic. Joey rang the bell.

The door flew open and a man stood there. He was in his mid-thirties. He was wearing an Ohio State T-shirt and holding a beer. There was the sound of a television blaring in the background. He looked us up and down. "What?" he said.

Joey explained the situation, how we were from Richmond, how we were headed for Dayton, how we'd hit something on the road and gotten a flat tire, how we had no jack or spare. The man sighed. He turned around and stared at his television. He looked down at his beer. He set the beer down. "Let me get my keys," he said.

His name was Dave. He drove us in his car—an old two-door Mustang—to a local garage where he knew the guy who drove the tow truck. The guy was missing his teeth and stared at me in a way I didn't like. He said the tow would cost one hundred dollars, and we told him we didn't have that kind of money. Dave drove us back to his house.

"You're sure you don't have a jack and a spare?" he said.

"We're sure," Joey said.

We helped Dave search through his garage for his own jack and an extra spare tire that he said belonged to a friend. He ran inside to check on the score of the game and then the three of us got back into his car and drove down to the highway. From the I-70 West, we passed our car on the opposite side of the road. We took the next exit and circled around and got on the highway once again, this time headed east. Dave kept the radio on low so he could listen to the game.

I kept apologizing. "We are so sorry to interrupt your day," I said.

"Yeah, man," Joey said unconvincingly. He knew nothing about sports. "I hope Ohio State wins big."

"Thanks," Dave said.

When we got back to the Calais, Dave popped the trunk and removed the gray flooring and there, in the tire well, were the spare and the jack.

"What are those doing in there?" Joey said. "Seriously." He looked at me. "Who knew there was a secret panel?"

Dave sighed and then kneeled down on the ground and jacked up the car. We stood a few feet away watching. After he changed the tire, we wrote down his address and thanked him again and promised to send him something for his trouble. "You have about eighty miles on that tire," he said. "More than enough to get you home."

He drove off in a cloud of muffler exhaust and we climbed back into the car.

"Should we go home?" I said.

"I guess. Of course, it's only twenty more miles to the mall. And then forty back home. That's only sixty." This was the only kind of math we were good at.

"That's true."

"We've still got time," Joey said. "The day is still young."

"And so are we," I said.

"An' I love it," he said. "So very, very much!"

We popped in Billy Idol, rewound "Rebel Yell" to the beginning, and headed east toward Dayton. (Eventually, all told, we drove another hundred miles all around Dayton on that little spare, which Joey nearly wore to the ground and which, his father later said, almost ruined the axle.)

"I just want you to know that the children are okay," Melanie Kraemer told my mother when she called her. This was how Mrs. Kraemer and my mom began most of their conversations with each other when Joey and I were out together: *There is nothing to worry about, but . . ."* *"Everything is going to be okay, but . . ."* *"The children are fine, but . . ."*

"They're fine and the car is fine," Mrs. Kraemer said now. "They called me from Dayton to say they'd had a flat tire, but that they got it changed and it's all okay. They decided that instead of coming home, they would just go on ahead with their plans."

"Of course they did," my mom said.

We'd only known each other three months when we discovered the Dayton Art Institute. It was a night when we were tired of Richmond and the usual people and parties. Joey picked me up in the red Calais and we put in Billy Idol and headed to Dayton, as fast as we could. The Institute sat on a hill overlooking the city with steps that lit up at night, and we sat on the highest one and looked out at all the lights. It was so open to the world, yet so removed from anyone who might know us. Joey smuggled vodka from his dad's liquor cabinet, which usually only contained Budweiser or Michelob Light, and we drank straight from the bottle and were cold in the winter wind. We pretended we liked the cold and pretended we liked the vodka. We got caught as a neighboring church let out and the congregation swept over us, Joey hiding the vodka under his XXXL shirt.

Afterward, we drove home fast to "Rebel Yell" and, back in Richmond, climbed a lonely train that sat in the factory yard outside the Purina building. It was just one boxcar that stood abandoned for some reason, as if it had been forgotten. We sat cross-legged on its roof and stared off down the tracks and out toward the high school, its spire lit up in the distance. From where we sat, the high school seemed less intimidating, less grand. Its halls were empty, its students scattered across town, some of them tucked in their houses, sleeping. We talked about what it would be like to some day leave Richmond far, far behind, and about all the places we would go.

Members of student congress: Bottom row—Jeff Shirazi, Ross Vigran, Danny Dickman, Tom Mangas, Ted Fox; Middle row—Robert Ignacio, Teresa Ripperger, Michele Long, Amy Johnson, Sarah Rosar, Beth Jennings, Michelle Zimmerman; Top row—Angie Oler, Ned Mitchell, Chris Jones

The Social Order

At least we're still best friends and we're not starving or Prince Charles or this girl I heard about on *Hard Copy* who was led into the woods by her two closest friends and then beaten to death with a log all because she was more popular than them. Thank God we weren't too popular. Just think what could have happened to us. Sherri Dillon and Tom Dehner might have enjoyed dropping us from the top of the Purina Tower.

—*Jennifer to Joey, December 10, 1992*

A ncient Egyptian society was structured like a pyramid. At the very top were the gods who controlled the universe. It was important to keep them happy because they could cause famine, make the Nile overflow, or bring on a horrible, grueling death. Pharaohs—human beings elevated to gods—were next in line. Below them were the nobles and priests, followed by the soldiers, the scribes, the merchants, the artisans, the farmers, and finally the slaves and servants.

Every society from the beginning of time has had a social order, from ants to bees to kings to pharaohs. Richmond High School was no different. We had our own complicated hierarchy just like any other high school. As soon as we arrived, we learned the rules.

Ranking was somewhat economic. Not usually racial. A cheerleader far outranked a Devilette drill team member. A football player outranked a tennis player. Some football players outranked others. The Richmond High School social structure was like some sort of invisible edict from God that dictated who was who in the order of things. Mostly it seemed random.

Joey and I set out to try to understand the great mystery of it all, and maybe, in doing so, figure out a way to become popular in the process. There was something we had discovered very early about ourselves and about each other: not only did we share a love for writing, a desire to do big things with our lives, and a need to move beyond our small town, but we wanted to be admired, to be liked, to belong, to do more than fit in: to be embraced.

The best way to try to sort it out was to break it down group by group, as if we were bees or Egyptians. We decided on Egyptians because they were easier and more exotic.

At the very top of the pyramid of the class of 1986 were

Teresa Ripperger (everyone called her "Rip") and Tom Dehner. Teresa played sports and was in student congress. She was fun and outgoing and gave the very best parties. Tom was a football player—good-looking, easygoing, smart. They had been going out since the sixth grade and moved in a stratosphere all their own. They were, quite clearly, the gods.

Below them, the cool kids (the pharaohs of the school) were made up of many of the jocks, almost all of the cheerleaders, and most of the members of student government. There were always exceptions, based on looks and personality. Having gone to Test Junior High School helped, of course, as did coming from money.

Then there were the soldiers—the normal kids—just trying to get by and do their work and live through high school. Sometimes they dated. Sometimes they didn't. Maybe they didn't date as much as they wished they could. They didn't always get asked to every dance or go to every dance. They didn't show up at parties, or maybe the parties they went to were somewhere other than Teresa's house. Or maybe, every once in a while, they did come to Rip's or to Tom Dehner's. The soldiers made up the majority of the school.

Next were the artisans—the drama nerds, the band fags, the orchestra and choir geeks. These were the diehards who lived for rehearsals, not those (like me) who merely showed up for class or performances and had other things to do with their time.

Then came the scribes, or brains. There were some who tried hard to be cool and to fit in, and some who didn't care to. There were brains who didn't have any social skills whatsoever but who were very good at math and science and computers. There were others who were so much smarter than everyone else that they had no choice but to be nerds.

The hoods (merchants) drove Camaros and Trans Ams, wore Black Sabbath or Iron Maiden T-shirts, and hung out in the Smokers Hall between classes. They took Auto Shop, and if they played sports, it was usually wrestling or baseball, sometimes football. They liked to cut class and were always in detention. Sometimes they were sexy in a bad and dangerous way. The female equivalent was girls with permed, platinum hair, the girls who put out, the ones who smoked openly and got pregnant and then dropped out of school before graduation.

The Special Ed students (farmers) were an assortment of sweet kids who weren't actually retarded but just a little slow; some who really were retarded; and a few lost causes like Johnnie Coons, the meanest girl I have ever known. We were in sixth grade together at Westview Elementary School and I was assigned to tutor her in reading. I will never forget sitting beside her in Mr. Shank's classroom while the rest of the class quietly read. She pulled out a switchblade and pressed it to my leg and said under her breath, "So help me God, if you teach me one word of reading, I will kill you." Each day, we sat there and she held the switchblade to my leg and I pretended to teach her to read, and when we graduated and went to Dennis Junior High School, they put her into the Special Ed class.

Somewhere off the pyramid, in a group all their own, were the few exchange students at our high school, usually Japanese girls. There was one boy from Turkey, a quiet, good-looking, dark-haired boy named Serdar Oğuz. We took AP History together and even though he never ever spoke, my other classmates and I had the impression that Serdar was very smart.

There was one more group that we hadn't worked in

anywhere: the kids who drifted from group to group—that's where Joey and I fit. We were liked but we also felt like outsiders, because in our eyes we were different, and the only reason we got along so well with everyone was because we adapted to them. We acted like support, like the beams of a building or the stone walls of a foundation, just as the nobles and the priests had so many years ago for the pharaohs and gods in ancient Egypt. We hung out with everybody. But we hung out mostly with each other.

Jennifer with neighborhood playmates

Why I Hate Girls

What girls do to each other is beyond description.
No Chinese torture comes close.

—*Tori Amos*

The problem with you," Joey said one day at lunch, "is that you want everyone to like you."

I said, "The problem with *me?*"

He said, "You're wasting your time on the cheerleaders. If you want them to like you, we have to go to the source. Teresa Ripperger. She's the one who decides what they think."

I said, "I don't care if they like me or not." And of course we both knew I was lying.

I tried to tell myself I was happy just being liked by some girls and by most of the boys. Wasn't that enough? After all, boys were more interesting and less catty. They didn't get upset if you received more attention than they did or if you were a threat to them in any way, and if they did get upset, they didn't let you know it because they didn't want to be made fun of. I always knew where I stood with boys. Besides, you could talk to boys about interesting things, not just hair and jeans and makeup.

But every time I suited up for gym class or stood in line behind the cheerleaders at lunch or ran into them at parties, I braced myself. I got nervous. I couldn't help it. I wanted them to like me or at least be nice to me.

I stood up to throw my lunch away. Joey said, "I'll wait for you over there." He pointed to the doors where Tom Dehner was leaning in his letter jacket, strong and manly, talking to Teresa.

I arrived at the trash can at the exact same moment as one of the cheerleaders. (*Does it really matter which one?* I thought, even as I started smiling—the stupid fake, nervous grin I always got around these girls. *Who can tell them apart?*) Her name was Staci or Traci or Tammi or Aimee. She said, "Hey."

I said, "Hey."

She shoved her trash into the can and held it open for me so I could do the same.

"Thanks," I said.

Just then Rob Jarrett walked by and winked at me. "What's up, McJunkin?" he said.

Staci/Traci watched him saunter off without turning her

head. Her eyes followed him right out the door. Some of the other cheerleaders walked up and immediately looked bored. Staci's eyes turned back to me. She said, "That's a cute shirt. Did you get it at Sears?"

The cheerleaders smiled then because everyone knew that was the last place on earth anyone would ever buy cute clothes. Staci might as well have said, "Did you dig that out of a Dumpster or steal it off a homeless person?"

Before I could say anything, she said, "I like your pants, too. I wish I was brave enough to wear pants with patterns, but I'm always worried they'll make my butt look big. I really admire your confidence."

Which, of course, translated to: "You must be insane or blind because the pants you're wearing make your butt look enormous."

And then she paraded off, followed by the others. I watched her go, unable to speak or move, and then I saw Joey waving to me. Tom Dehner was gone and so was Teresa. Even Tommy Wissel was gone, which meant we were going to be late for class.

Later that day, before sixth period, Staci was leaving the downstairs central hall bathroom as I was walking in. She fake smiled at me and I fake smiled at her. I shut myself in one of the bathroom stalls and calmed myself down. I breathed as deeply as I could, given that I was in a bathroom. Then I saw it. On the back of the door there was a new entry written in red Magic Marker: *Jennifer McJunkin is a ho-bag.* The ink was still wet.

I thought back to the student handbook I had thrown away my first week of school, trying to remember the punishment for defacing school property. I pulled a purple Magic Marker from my bag and ran it back and forth, fast as I could, across the writing until it was just a big, messy purple blob. Afterward, I threw the marker in the trash.

I went home that night and put on my stereo head-phones (Fleetwood Mac's *Tusk,* the album I always listened to when I was feeling upset or lonely or blue) and sat in my green beanbag and cried. I couldn't help it. I told myself it wasn't personal, it wasn't just me. Girls were always hateful to other girls. But it felt personal. I was *not* a ho-bag. The sluttiest thing I'd ever done was kiss my ex-boyfriend Brian Yoder, and we hadn't even used our tongues (we'd kept our mouths closed, afraid of getting our braces tangled up).

I decided I wanted to go to boarding school like some of my friends whose parents worked at Earlham with my dad. A lot of the Earlham kids I knew went off to Quaker board-ing school for high school—to fine, academic institutions in the Northeast where students no doubt acted like real people and not mean and soulless creatures—but I didn't want to leave my parents or my cats or my dog or my room (which I didn't have to share with anyone else) or Joey. The thought of leaving made me cry even harder. I was such a baby. Here I was, the Great Ho-Bag of the Bathroom Stall, and all I wanted was my mommy.

The next morning I put on plain pants with no pattern and one of my nicest shirts, which I clearly hadn't bought at Sears. At lunch, I avoided Staci. I didn't even look in her direction. When I got up to throw away my food, a good-looking senior named Rod Ogren followed me to the trash can and asked me out for Saturday night. As we made plans to go to the movies, I thought, *Who needs girls?* I decided to wait on boarding school, at least for the time being.

From *The Pierian,* the 1984
Richmond High School Yearbook . . .

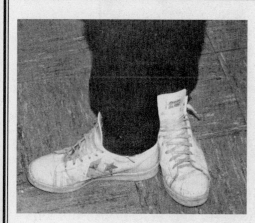

What's Out

OUT

Country music, valley girls, leg warmers, bell-bottom jeans, preppies, pink hair, Izods, mohawk haircuts, Dallas Cowboys, morals, saddle shoes, the Go-Go's, disco mini skirts, knickers, Blondie, the new attendance policy, Converse tennis shoes, long hair, French braids, homework, E.T., herpes, designer jeans, Pac-man, prairie skirts, Mr. T, anything generic, "fer sure," and punk rockers

What's In

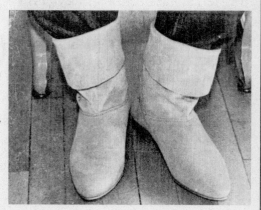

Leather and chains, pierced ears, Prince, baggies, bright colors, being "scared," bandanas, porno, break dancing, videos, L.A. Raiders, vans, concerts, thin ties, blue-jean jackets, Quiet Riot, Peter Pan boots, Rock-n-Roll, hats, British men, parties, the *Flashdance* look, pinstripe jeans, parachute pants, curly hair, the Nautilus, Ocean Pacific, oriental writing, and sports cars.

Jennifer, her big hair, and her pearls

Dress Code

Only because I'm in love, I'm getting R.'s picture, there's a chance I'll get some hair spray next hour, and the fact that we're not writing in here today has saved you! But you're not forgiven! Especially if R. stops liking me because my hair is flat!

—*Jennifer to Laura Lonigro, writing about the impossible*

I was determined from the beginning of high school to be known as a fashion plate, as someone off a New York runway. Unfortunately, living in Richmond made this challenging because our town was, sadly, a good fifty to sixty years behind the times.

There were several places in Richmond to get your hair cut or styled: Le Crazy Horse, Fiesta Hair Fashions, the Golden Shears, the Hair Event, the Hair Hut, the Hairport, Jenny's Cut and Curl, Top O' the Head, and Wanda's Beauty Salon—"Watch our hands create heads of beauty." My mother and I went to Ova's Hairum, which was just off the pedestrian shopping area, the Promenade, downtown. As my mom said, the name was too good *not* to go there.

Richmond was home to two popular beauty schools where many of my classmates would apply after graduation: Amber's Beauty School ("Serving this area since 1936") and P.J.'s College of Cosmetology ("Your future begins with us"). There was a Merle Norman Cosmetic Studio on the Promenade (which ran the length of several downtown blocks), and clothing stores like the Fashion Bug, the Secret Ingredient, Maurice's, and Peggy's Youthful Fashions for the Fuller Figure.

Even with this, people still wore feathered hair, parted down the middle. The mullet was popular. So was Jheri Curl. There were rattails and perms. Fluorescent colors. Leg warmers. Belted sweaters. Ripped sweatshirts. Izods in all colors with the collars turned up. Penny loafers. "Frankie Say Relax" shirts. I had even seen more than one pair of bell-bottoms, even though the 1970s were long over.

I told my parents I would rather be caught dead than shop on the Promenade or at the Richmond Square Mall. It was bad enough I had to live in Richmond, but did I have to dress like everyone else, too? I wanted to fit in, but not completely, not in this way. I needed to express my individuality, and I was very into clothes. My father, who also had a passion for clothing, understood. He never shopped in town. When it was time to buy my school wardrobe, he made sure we went to Cincinnati or Chicago or Indianapolis or New York or, at the very least, Dayton.

We came back to school in January 1984 after winter break. It had been an especially wonderful Christmas and I was wearing my new favorite outfit—a yellow Esprit long-sleeved shirt with gray and white stripes that almost reached my knees. Over it, I wore a little black vest I'd found at a vintage store, and under it I wore a new Esprit skirt with tights and boots. The whole thing was quite groovy and cool and I felt like fashion icon Lisa Bonet or a glamorous person right off the streets of New York. I loved Esprit. I could have moved into the Esprit department at the Dayton Mall and been happy forever. It was true I was being imprisoned in this town—temporarily—but I was not of it, and I knew it and so would everyone else.

My hair, no longer feathered like Jaclyn Smith's, was large and curly (even curlier than its natural curl), thanks to the two hours I'd spent that morning blowing it dry and rolling it with hot rollers, then teasing it and spraying it with Aqua Net. I was wearing shiny blue-gray eye shadow and three different shades of lipstick (no one shade ever gave me the color I wanted), and over that a coating of Bonne Bell lip gloss. All I needed was a soundtrack—something sexy by Blondie or Sheila E—and I was like something out of a movie.

I was walking down the main long hallway with Joey and Hether Rielly, fighting and shoving our way through the sea of people, and we were talking over one another and laughing. I was also keeping an eye out for any boys I liked so that

I could say hi to them or (hopefully) smile at them and have them say hi to me first. This was a very deliberate activity that I tried to make look easy and natural, like I wasn't giving it any thought at all. I knew the class schedules and, therefore, hallway schedules of all the guys I had crushes on, so I knew when to watch out for them. Right now I was looking for my favorite, Dean Waldemar, who was with no exaggeration a golden god, and who should just be coming up from the swimming pool at any minute, his hair still wet.

So I was walking and talking and laughing and saying hi, all the while looking out for Dean, when suddenly—at the other end of that long hallway, coming down the steps from the cafeteria area—I caught sight of something that looked strangely familiar. It was a yellow something with gray and white stripes.

When I stopped talking, Joey and Hether looked at me. "What's wrong?" Hether said.

"I just saw something . . ."

The yellow was gone. It had disappeared into the crowd. I was trying to find it again. Joey and Hether looked with me, but since they didn't know what I was looking for, they gave up.

"What are we looking at?" Joey said.

"Nothing," I said. "I'm just seeing things."

We went on, heading for the central stairs. When we got there, my shirt was coming toward me—my new favorite Christmas Esprit shirt that I was wearing right that very moment. Yellow with gray and white stripes. It was walking right at me on Patty Boomershine, who was big and tough and who smoked cigarettes and hung around in the parking lot after school sometimes and shouted mean things at people just because she was bored. Underneath the shirt she was wearing ratty old jeans and sneakers. With Magic Marker, she had written "Fuck" on the knee of one leg and "off!" on the other.

Joey said, "Holy shit." Joey kept a clothing journal to help him keep track of what he wore. This was so he didn't repeat an outfit in three weeks' time.

Date

Tues.: Brown Saturday sweater; blue/white stripe safari, generic blue pants, penny loafers.

Weds.: New blue sweats; blue/green new Izod oxford, tennis shoes.

Thurs.: Maroon argyle. White shirt. Lee jeans. Maroon tennis.

Fri.: Old navy blue sweatshirt; Maroon/gray/green-striped Izod; old 501's.

Sat.: Speech meet. D's green sports coat/sports tie, white shirt, loafers.

Sun.: (Veteran's Day weekend) Good reddish sweats; genera pants; M's blue/white shirt. Nite: (drunk again @ Rip's) M's red Izod sweatshirt, old 501's.

Mon.: (HUNGOVER) Gray sweats; M's IU sweatshirt.

When we could, Hether and I would break into Joey's room and steal his journal and change things here or there so that he would get confused and accidentally wear something twice in a row or repeat an outfit before he was supposed to. We would always tell him afterward, of course, just so we could see his reaction.

Hether said now, "Jenna Lou Anne, that bitch is wearing your shirt."

I said, "Turn me around. Turn me around." Because suddenly I couldn't move and there were five thousand people coming—including Dean Waldemar, who I could just see heading toward me (gold hair dripping wet) surrounded by ten of his closest friends—and I didn't want to see them or Patty or anyone.

Patty said, "Jennifer McJunkin, oh my God."

I said, "Hi, Patty."

She said, "Look at this. You and me're twins."

I said, "Yeah!" I stood there grinning stupidly, wanting to slink away to the bathroom or maybe just die instantly on the spot. Guys and girls were walking by staring at us and laughing. "Nice shirts!" they said. "Hey, is it Spirit Week?" someone yelled. "Is today Twin Day?" I saw Dean Waldemar straining to see what everyone was looking at. I was already thinking about what to do, trying to remember if I had anything to change in to. Could I get away with only wearing my vest or maybe my ugly gym uniform?

Joey said, "We'd better go. We'll be late!" And started dragging me off. My legs weren't working anymore so I kind of bumped along behind him.

The rest of the day, I darted from class to class, keeping one eye out for Patty, the other for anyone who might have seen us together. This was the worst thing to happen to me since the time just before Christmas when Mike Shockney made me laugh so hard in Psychology that something flew out of my nose and landed on his book. (I pretended, of course, that nothing happened. Just picked up my pencil and started furiously taking notes, hoping to God he wouldn't notice. He was very good-looking for a hood.)

I went home that day and took off my shirt. Instead of throwing it onto the floor or my beanbag chair with my other clothes, I hung it neatly on a hanger and pushed it into the very back of my closet. I didn't wear it again until I graduated high school and was safely out of Richmond. As far as I was concerned, that shirt belonged to Patty Boomershine. She wore it once a week for the next two and a half years.

On the way to Dayton from Richmond on the I-70

Cafeteria Rules

Jennifer has had a great week at school. She is a great authority on all the Kindergarten rules, such as Keep Your Head in the School Bus and I Shouldn't Have to Scream to Get Your Attention!

—My mother in a letter to the family, September 11, 1973

Technically, RHS was a closed campus, which meant we had to stay at school no matter what, even if we were dying, and never leave it until the final bell rang at 3:15. No one paid attention to this, of course, except the dutiful kids and the ones who were trying for the perfect attendance award. At lunch, it was easy enough to slip out through the art museum and walk down to Rax, on the corner of National Road West and Red Devil Boulevard, or to hop into your car and drive to Burger King or Wendy's or McDonald's.

Hether Rielly and Joey Kraemer and I had the same lunch hour second semester sophomore year, which meant that we almost never ate at school and were always sneaking out. Hether usually drove because we loved her red Cougar. She drove faster than anyone in the world, even my own father who almost always got a ticket every time we left the house. Hether just slammed her foot on the gas pedal and didn't let up till we got to wherever we were going.

One particularly restless and dull day in April, in AP History class first period, Joey wrote me a note. He said, *I am bored out of my mind. I'm close to dying. I mean it. Let's do something different for lunch today.*

I wrote back and said: *Where do you want to go?*

He said: *Anywhere but here.*

Rax?

No.

Burger King?

No.

Wendy's?

Yes. In Dayton!

You are crazy. And doesn't Todd Irwin look good today? Todd was lean and tall and had brown hair that used to be straight but now was curly. He was going out with Leigh Torbeck, who was a cheerleader. They were one of *those* couples who you knew would be together forever and would never ever break up no matter how much you wanted them to, which meant I would never have a chance with Todd myself. But I still thought he was cute.

Joey wrote: *Hether can drive. We'll be back in time for 5th period. I just have to get out of this town.*

We met Hether after fourth hour in the Orchestra Hall and the three of us walked down the ramp and past the choir room, the art rooms, the orchestra and band room, and out the back door. Hether's car was parked illegally in the side parking lot where she always parked it.

We got in—Joey in the backseat, me in the front, Hether behind the wheel—and peeled out, music blasting, something loud and rebellious. It was a white-hot sunny day, warm for April. We rolled the windows down, and for once I thought to hell with my hair.

Hether slammed her foot down on the gas and aimed the Cougar toward Dayton. We flew past the Courthouse, past the Promenade, past Glen Miller Park, past the Arboretum, past Target, past the Richmond Square Mall, past Fred First Ford, past the Spirit of 76 Motel, and then out onto I-70 and east under the giant light blue Ohio arch.

"Let's see how fast we can go, big girl!" Joey shouted over the music.

We had just under an hour to get there and back before fifth period. It was forty miles to Dayton from Richmond one-way. Hether accelerated and we screamed. She said, "Hold on!!!" The speedometer climbed past 70 to 80, 85, 90, 95, and finally hovered just over 100. Joey and I started dancing wildly.

There was a Wendy's near the airport exit, and that was the one we were aiming for. We knew we wouldn't have time to go inside and eat, so we would just zip on through the drive-through. In about twenty-five minutes, we saw the sign.

"There!" I hollered.

Hether careened across three lanes (there wasn't much traffic) and raced off the exit. We pulled up to the drive-through where there wasn't any line. We ordered three Frosties, three cheeseburgers, and three orders of fries. And then we pulled around to the window and waited. We sat there looking at one another. We looked like we'd been caught in a tornado, our hair sticking up and out in every direction. Hether's face was red like it always was when she laughed too hard or got too excited. Joey was grinning wickedly. I realized I was out of breath from dancing and screaming. I stretched my legs up and put them on the dash. Suddenly I didn't care if we went back or if Mr. Wysong marked us absent. I wanted to keep driving just as fast as we could.

Hether handed us the Frosties and the cheeseburgers and the fries and we divvied everything up. Then she hit the gas and peeled out of the parking lot, pointed toward home. "Hold on!!!" she shouted. We were like a bright red rocket taking off across a backdrop of cornfields and silos and barns and farmhouses. We passed tractors and semitrailers and a car or two, but never a cop. Where were they all?

We made it back to school in under twenty-five minutes, with the whole trip clocking in at exactly one hour, which we were sure was a world's record. Hether and I slid into Humanities class, hair wild, faces red, clothes askew, just as the bell was ringing. Everyone stared. Mr. Wysong quirked an eyebrow at us and one corner of his mouth shot up. He said, "Ladies. Nice of you to join us."

"Thank you," I said.

We sat at the back of the room. Todd Irwin was on my other side. I bent down to get my notebook and my pen. I wiped the ketchup off my shoe and smoothed my hair.

Mr. Wysong was already droning on at the board.

Todd leaned over and said, "What the hell have you been doing, Jennifer?"

I said, "Oh, we went to Wendy's for lunch." He nodded and sat back in his chair. I couldn't decide whether I liked him better with straight hair or curly hair. I thought he looked cute either way. "In *Dayton*." I smiled at Todd. His eyes widened and the look he gave me—one of surprise, wonder, and just the slightest bit of admiration—was worth the entire trip.

Jennifer and Eric Lundquist

First Love

Who are my current romantic interests? Well, there are several, I'm afraid. They are as follows: Greg Embry, Kenny Gibbs, Tom Mangas, Alex Delaney, Mike Bullerdick, Jeff Schwartz, Matt Ashton, Mitch Gaylord (Olympic gymnast gold medalist), and the lead singer of the music group Wham!

—*My diary, December 25, 1984*

Teresa Ripperger and Tom Dehner fell in love when they were twelve. They grew up two houses away from each other in Reeveston, and they arrived at RHS as the sophomore power couple, becoming king and queen of our class. Considering that Rip (as Teresa was called) wasn't a cheerleader, this was amazing. She wasn't feminine or girly, but she was tall and athletic and gregarious and attractive, and she liked to have a good time. The activities she excelled in were socializing and giving really good parties, and (practically) everyone loved her, especially Tom, who was the boy we all admired most.

Tom was a football player. He was laid-back, smart, and always wore a kind of dreamy, crooked smile. Red hair ran in his family. His older brother John was tall and lean and had dark red hair that he parted down the middle. Tom wasn't quite as tall, wasn't quite as lean, and his hair was more of a golden brown with hints of red. It curled in the humidity and he had freckles. His face was broad and square. He wasn't the best-looking boy in our class (that would be Rob Jarrett) or the most charismatic (Tom Mangas) or the funniest (Tommy Wissel), but there was something about him that drew us to him. He was Mr. All-American. He was a genuinely nice guy. He was sexy, but still approachable.

We thought Tom and Teresa were the perfect couple. They were who we all aspired to be. Every now and then there was trouble, but only for a day or two, and usually because there were other girls chasing after Tom. He was so friendly (some said a little *too* friendly) that he never really turned them away, and Rip would get mad and yell at him by his locker, which was right outside Mr. Alexander's room. Mr. Alexander taught English and was the best-looking teacher at RHS. He had dark hair and was very tan and always wore nice suits. When Teresa was yelling at Tom, Mr. Alexander would come outside and ask her to keep it down. She always shut up and walked away and then told everyone that she was going to kill those little bitches who were trying to steal Tom from her.

The next day, Rip and Dehner would be walking down

the halls together once again and the rest of us would swoon. If only we could find a love like that—so passionate, so forgiving, so steadfast and true, so obviously meant to be, so *forever*. If only we could be so lucky.

Eric Lundquist played trombone in the Richmond High School band. He had broad shoulders and tan skin and shiny gold-brown hair and dimples on both cheeks. He was a sophomore like I was, and his father was a chemistry teacher at the high school. I was copresident of the speech team, just as I had been in junior high, and Eric came to one of our first meetings. That was how we met.

Eric had a girlfriend named Carrie Hockersmith who was a year older than we were. She wore skirts that came to her ankles and little barrettes that pinned back her hair on either side of her face. She worked after school and on weekends in the shoe department at Elder-Beerman, the downtown department store, and had been sewing since the seventh grade. She was the 4-H Grand Sewing Champion for two years running.

Eric and I fell in love on a single long speech team bus ride. Until that point, we had been exchanging glances and talking during speech meetings and Spanish class, but on that bus ride he sat in front of me, turned sideways in his seat, one golden arm resting casually across the top of it, and we talked the entire time. He was the first boy (other than Joey) that I could really talk to, who really listened. We talked about everything—speech and school and books and life. We laughed and laughed. I liked the way his dimples showed around his mouth when he smiled. Being around him made me feel warm and happy from deep inside. By the end of the bus ride, we both knew we were meant to be.

Eric broke up with Carrie, who took it badly. She wrote him notes, asking him to get back together, and gave me nasty, threatening looks. Once, when I was shopping at Elder-Beerman, she left all her customers and walked out of the store. I hated her and was jealous of her because she'd been with Eric first and for a long time. She hated me even more because I was with him now.

Eric and I started going together on October 13, 1983. We bought matching red sweaters and had them embroidered with "RHS" in white cursive. We wore these to speech meets, and I also wore my favorite painter's cap that said "Why Be Normal?" We sat in the back of the speech team bus, huddled under our coats, and held hands and kissed.

We went on dates to the movies and the mall. I spent hours getting ready—working on my hair, my makeup, deciding what to wear. I changed clothes a hundred times. Eric's father drove us in his station wagon and my dad drove us in his silver Mercedes, when it was running. I liked the Mercedes, even though it must have been at least twenty years old and it barely worked. The insides were leather and chrome and smelled like my dad's pipe, and there was a sun roof you could open if you had enough arm strength and patience.

We went on group dates—to basketball games and football games, to dances. One night early in the fall of our sophomore year, we had a couples party in the family room in our basement as part of a plan to find my friend Kelley Robertson a boyfriend and get her to fall in love with David Anthony, who was geeky but cute, and to get him to fall in love with her. Kelley, who was not only my friend but my neighbor, and I had spent the better part of a weekend and after school creating an elaborate board game full of seductive activities such as "Kiss on the couch," or "Five minutes in the water heater closet with the person of your choice."

We had movie and television dates at my house, in our basement family room, which was private, even though my parents were always lurking about, and which had a fireplace and a large, comfortable couch. Eric and I sat close together and watched *The Love Boat* and kissed. We had dates at his house that sometimes began with me reading aloud to his entire family from a story that Joey and I had written together—usually a short story about an elf who murdered people by stuffing them into washing machines or a repressed librarian who was secretly into patron bondage. Eric's father and mother and his sister Beth were quiet, churchgoing people. They sat listening politely and attentively, trying not to look confused or horrified, while Eric beamed as if I was reciting one of Shakespeare's sonnets.

These dates ended in my basement or, more rarely, in his basement den, which was only partially finished and had a work space for his dad with lots of chemistry-type beakers and bottles. Toward the back of his basement was a blackboard that acted as a wall, and a large oval corded rug on a concrete floor, and Eric and I lay there and experimented with things beyond kissing.

Lying on that rug with Eric, or on the couch in my basement, my head spun and my heart beat so fast that I felt like I was going to throw up, kind of like I always did just after getting off a roller coaster at King's Island. But it was a kind of dreamy feeling, too, very light and lovely. Afterward, I locked myself in my green room and read *Our Bodies, Ourselves*, a book my mom had gotten me years earlier, trying to figure out what was happening to me.

Sometimes Eric and I walked in the woods and the field

across from his house and held hands. We lay down in the grass and looked up at the blue sky and talked about everything we could think of, and other times we just lay there in silence, touching arms. I wanted it to always be that way— beautiful and breathtaking and innocent and painful all at once.

One day I took a permanent marker and drew an enormous smiley face on the blackboard in his basement because it was how I felt inside. Eric walked me to class and wrote me notes and we talked on the phone for hours at night. He learned all my secrets and all my dreams, and for a long time we were very happy.

After Eric and I had been together for seven months, Joey started giving me his advice about the situation. He thought I should move on and date someone more exciting, someone like Todd Irwin or Jeff Shirazi, who played football like Todd and drove a red VW Bug convertible and had black hair that fell across his forehead and sexy blue eyes. Joey thought I should save myself for Tom Dehner, in case he ever became a free man. Besides, he wanted more time with me himself. Our friendship was already leaning toward exclusivity. We spoke a language no one else really understood. We finished each other's sentences. We were, we said, separated at birth, and no one, not even Eric, could come between us.

In June 1984, two weeks after school let out for summer and sophomore year ended, my mom and I drove to North and South Carolina as we always did, to visit her parents and my dad's parents and all of my aunts and uncles and cousins. The night before, Eric and I said a tearful good-bye and he gave me the shirt off his back to remember him by. We hugged and kissed and then I saw, out of the corner of my eye, two bodies—one enormous and dark, the other slight and blond—crouching behind the bushes by the front door.

Ross Vigran and Joey were like the annoying brothers I never had, always spying on me. Ross was one of the only Jewish people in our school. He had gone to Test and lived in Reeveston with his parents, both of whom were practically giants. There were rumors of older brothers who had already graduated from high school—bigger, taller older brothers. At six foot three, two-hundred-some pounds, Ross was the youngest and the smallest.

When Eric pulled the shirt off his back and handed it to me, telling me to wear it over the next few weeks to remember him by, I heard Ross snort. After Eric left, climbing into his dad's green station wagon, I let them have it for ruining such a beautiful moment for me.

"Just what the hell do you think you're doing?"

Joey and Ross scrambled out of the bushes like dogs. "Oh, Jennifer, here's my shirt." Ross started to pull up his XXXL polo.

"No, take mine," Joey said. He also wore an XXXL polo, but not because he needed to. He just liked the roomy fit of it.

"You all are terrible."

Ross was bent double, wiping the tears from his eyes. His face was the dark red color it always turned when he laughed hard. He loved to cause trouble and to stir people up. He lived for it.

"I mean it. I'm not speaking to either one of you again."

"It was all Ross's idea, of course," said Joey. "But while we're here. When *are* you going to dump him?"

• • •

Eric went to band camp and then settled in to work at Hayes Regional Arboretum, all 355 acres of it, while I made the rounds of relatives in the Carolinas. The first few nights of my trip, I slept in his shirt, inhaling him—a familiar, heady mix of shampoo, Polo cologne, and the great, earthy outdoors.

One week later, I was in love with Matthew Ashton again. We were in Greer, South Carolina, staying with my aunt Lynn and my uncle Phil and my cousins Lisa, Shannon, and Derek. Matt was a friend of Derek's. I had met him the previous summer, before I ever knew Eric. He looked like Scott Baio and was one year older than I was. He was, according to Derek, the coolest guy at Riverside High. We had dated and kissed and written each other letters, but then I'd met Eric, and Matt had met the girl of his dreams, and we stopped writing to each other. But suddenly, here he was and here I was and he still looked like Scott Baio.

Eric kept his promise and wrote me, if not daily at least every couple of days. I wrote him back, careful not to mention Matt. Eric copied down the lyrics to our song—Journey's "Faithfully"—and sent them to me.

It was horrible. I was riddled with guilt. I could barely sleep at night, and when I did, my dreams were filled with images of a hurt and furious Eric, tearing his shirt into little pieces and throwing them back into my face. Clearly, something was wrong with me that I could feel so much so quickly for someone else. I still loved Eric, but I loved Matt, too.

On the car ride back to Indiana at the end of the summer, I listened to my Walkman and agonized. Madonna's "Crazy for You." Chicago's "Hard Habit to Break." Journey's "Faithfully." And just to torture myself, Hall & Oates's "Maneater," which clearly had been written about me. I wondered if I would ever be able to marry one day, to be faithful to one person, to settle down. I wondered how I could ever break Eric's heart when he loved me, when I still loved him. Then I remembered Matt Ashton and the thought of him made me light-headed. Finally, I rested my head back against the seat and closed my eyes. Love was exhausting.

When I got home to Indiana, Eric was waiting for me. We talked my first night back and made plans to see each other the next day. When Eric showed up at my house in his dad's green station wagon, I met him on the front porch with the shirt he had given me weeks before. He looked happy to see me. His face lit up and he hugged me hard and tight so that the breath squeezed out of me and for a long time I couldn't breathe. He smelled good and clean and I wanted to inhale him, but at the same time he was too good, too clean, and I wanted him to go away.

When we finally broke apart, he could tell something was wrong. "What is it?" he said. "Did something happen on your trip?"

"Yes," I said. We sat down on the front step, side by side, legs touching. I didn't know what to say after that. He took my hand. It felt familiar and warm. It was a hand that made me want to hold on to it and tell it secrets and dreams and lean on it and not let it go. I said, "I realized while I was gone that I need some space. We can still date, but we can't go together anymore. We can see each other, but I think we need to see other people, too."

Eric dropped my hand and stared at me. He shook his head over and over. He said, "I don't understand."

So I told him again and again and again. It was horrible and ugly and sad, and Eric still didn't understand. Afterward I felt like I'd just destroyed something priceless and precious.

Eric tried for weeks to change my mind. He showed up at our house at odd hours. We stood on my porch in the middle of the night under the lone lightbulb, his usually bright face gloomy and serious. He said, "Why are you doing this? What happened? What can I do to get you back?"

I could barely look at him. I stared at his feet, at my feet. I said, "It isn't you. It's me. I still love you, but I'm too young to be tied down. I can't be so serious right now."

He said, "It sounds like Joey talking, not you. Or someone else. This doesn't sound like the Jennifer I know."

I said, "It is me. It's all me. I just can't do this. It's too much." And the more we talked, the angrier I got. I just wanted him to go away so that he wouldn't make me hurt him anymore.

At school, I did my best to avoid him. And the next time he came to my house late at night, my mother went out to talk to him instead. I never went downstairs again when I knew Eric was at the door. I just stayed upstairs in my room, looking out the window, down on his gold-brown head, while Mom went out to console him and send him home.

At the end of it all, we stopped speaking altogether. I was alternately flattered by his devotion and angry at his persistence. *How dare he try to hold me down when I am so young and vital and full of life*, I wrote in the on-again, off-again diary I kept. *How dare he try to tie me down in the prime of my life!*

I was dating Tom Mangas again when Eric began going with Nancy Bohlander, who also played in the band and was a member of the Devilettes drill team. Tom was easy and fun. He was exciting. We liked to go to the movies and then go parking sometimes at the abandoned Starr Piano Factory lot in his big old Buick Electra. Tom was smart and charismatic. But he never wanted a commitment. I didn't have to worry about being tied down with him. I didn't have to worry about things being too intense. I could still like Matt Ashton. I could still like other boys. I could still feel free if I wanted to.

Nancy Bohlander was skinny and had short fuzzy brown hair and a sour face that looked squished, as if someone had squeezed it from either side. In many ways, Nancy was much more suited for Eric than I had ever been because they could talk about band things. It didn't matter that I was dating one of the coolest boys in our class or that I had broken up with Eric, I went home to my green room and felt sorry for myself. Eric had learned to love again. I had been so sure he was going to love me forever, even if he couldn't have me. I had thought he would always be standing there on the steps outside my house, asking me to come back to him.

I lay down flat on top of the clothes that were always piled on my green floor (it was too much trouble to hang them up) and ignored all of Joey's calls and Tom's calls and Ross's calls. Instead, I turned on my stereo, pulled on my headphones, and listened to ABBA. I listened to "The Winner Takes It All" over and over again, and then I copied down the lyrics on a sheet of paper.

The next day at school, I walked past Eric's desk after Spanish class and handed the piece of paper to him. I tried to look as tragic as I felt. I kept my eyes cast down. I wanted Eric to know how hurt I was. Nancy Bohlander waited for him after class and I marched by her without saying a word.

When he tried to talk to me about it later, I told him I couldn't, that I was too distraught. I told him I didn't think it was completely over between us, and I just couldn't believe he would give up so easily. He was frustrated and confused and I could tell he didn't know whether to shake me or kiss me.

Soon after, I stopped dating Tom and started dating Jon Jerman, a hood. Every day, I walked to gym class through the Smokers Hall just so I could see him. This was not a boy who would make you tapes or copy down lyrics for you. He was lean and taut, with long, feathered hair the color of wheat, and sleepy blue eyes. He wore heavy metal T-shirts, the kind with the black three-quarter-length sleeves—his favorite said *Metallica*, a band I'd barely heard of. The hardest band I listened to was Cheap Trick, up in my green room with my yellow canopy bed. I knew Jon drove a black Trans Am and that he stared at me every time I walked past. Each time I walked by him, and when he took me out, I felt I was doing something very dangerous, something I never would have done before, when I was going with Eric and we were lying in the field outside his house staring up at the blue, blue sky.

Jennifer on her green telephone

The Telephone

We loved the telephone, and if the words which passed between 962-3827 and 966-1666 might be weighed, I think a globe might wobble beneath the tonnage. We talked about all the many things we wanted to be, on those nights when the moon was out and parties were high, but we were alone together on the phone.

—Joey to Jennifer

Iwas convinced my dad lived to humiliate me, that he lay in bed at night thinking up new and devious ways to mortify me in front of my friends and boyfriends.

One of the worst ways was the telephone. For some reason, we had five telephones in our house. Whenever one rang, I threw myself at it. On the rare occasion my dad answered it before I could, he used one of several hundred fake accents he saved up just for this purpose. My father had studied South Asian history and languages in undergraduate and graduate school, and because of this was semifluent in languages like Hindi and Urdu and, from his army days, Japanese. The ones he didn't know he faked. My friends would either hang up without saying anything or leaving a message, or just sit there on the phone in stunned silence.

Several of the boys I went to school with ended up in the local jail at one time or another. These weren't boys I hung around with usually, but I knew of them—we all knew of them—so when one of them started calling me collect from the Wayne County Jail, I sort of vaguely knew who it was.

"This is a collect call for Jennifer McJunkin from Bobby Watts. Will you accept the charges?"

The first time it happened, I said yes because I didn't know why he was calling me. I only knew Bobby in a roundabout way—he was an upperclassman on the football team who sometimes showed up at parties at Devon Johnson's house. Even then, I couldn't really picture his face.

"Okay," I said.

There was static on the line and then a deep male voice. "Hey. What's going on?"

"Uh, nothing much. What are you doing?"

"Just chillin'. I hope you don't mind me calling. I was trying to get up my nerve. Your picture looked good in the yearbook."

"Thank you." I had no idea what to say to him.

"So what's goin' on?"

"Just school. You know. Homework. Hanging out." Should I talk about the history team or the essay I'd written for Advanced Comp. on shopping? Would he be interested in hearing about the speech team or Ian Barnes's last party?

"That's cool. Well, I gotta go back to my cell. Can I call you again?" I didn't know what to say. I wanted to say no, but he was a convict. I didn't want to make him mad. I didn't even know what he was in for. What if he broke out and came to find me and killed me because I told him not to call me? I was standing in the kitchen. I looked out now at the dark, dark woods that surrounded our backyard.

"Um, sure," I said, thinking I'd just let my dad answer the phone for a while.

"Okay. Bye. You stay sweet."

"Thanks," I said. "You, too."

I hung up the phone and went to the cabinet to search for the Joy Ann cookies in the special hiding place Mom and I had from Dad—way up on the top shelf, behind some old cookbooks and napkins no one ever looked at or used. Mom wandered into the kitchen. "Who was that?"

"Some boy I go to school with."

"Asking you out?"

"I don't think so. He was calling from jail." Which, of course, was the wrong thing to say to my mother, who wanted to know how he got our number from prison and were they just handing out numbers of young girls to inmates and letting them make phone calls to every girl in town, and however I felt about it I needed to let my father answer the phone from now on, etc. As she talked, I ate my butter crunch cookie—best in the world—and felt a little thrill. I would have to get the yearbook out to remember who Bobby

Watts even was exactly, so the thrill wasn't about him at all. There was just something about prisons.

Ross Vigran called me one night and said, "Guess where I'm calling you from?"

I said, "Your room." Because this was always where Ross called me from.

He said, "No. Guess again."

Ross liked people to guess things, which was very annoying. He would make you keep guessing until you either guessed whatever it was or lost your mind.

I said, "No."

Because I either sounded like I meant business or because he was too excited to wait for me to guess, he said, "I'm in my front yard."

I said, "What?"

He said, "I'm on a cordless phone."

This was a very big deal and I was very, very envious. I wanted to get my own hands on a cordless phone right that minute—just the idea of a phone without limits, of one that you could talk on anywhere. I wondered if Target was still open, even though I wouldn't be caught dead in a Target because it was in Richmond and Richmond people shopped there and they didn't sell Esprit.

I said, "No you're not."

He said, "Wanna bet?" And he rustled around a little in what sounded like leaves, making outdoor-type noises.

I paced around my room, twisting the phone cord as I went. Ross told me all about his cordless phone, and after we had finally exhausted everything there was to say about it, we moved on to other subjects—his ex-girlfriend Tally (they had just broken up), my boyfriend Alex, the upcoming football game, Teresa's party. Ross was still sad about Tally and I was mostly trying to cheer him up.

Suddenly there was some sort of static on the line. We both heard it. "What's that?" I said. It sounded almost like a voice. It was fuzzy and hard to make out. We stopped talking and listened. Static-static. Fuzz-fuzz.

"I don't know," Ross said.

We went back to talking. A few minutes later, Ross said, "Hold on a minute." We listened again. This time there was no static or fuzz.

A voice—thin and clear, though far away, came over the phone from somewhere else: "Tally dumped Ross's ass, but he's telling everyone they broke up with each other and that they both wanted it." There was wild laughter.

I said, "Is that Cliff?" Cliff Lester lived across the street from Ross. He was the only person I knew except for Ross to have a cordless phone. (Cliff had everything before anyone else—a convertible, MTV, HBO, call-waiting.)

Ross said, "I'll call you right back." And hung up the phone.

I sat down on my floor and waited, my heart racing. I tried to picture Cliff's face when Ross called him. Cliff, of course, would click over because he had call-waiting. And there would be Ross, who had heard everything Cliff said . . .

The phone rang. I grabbed it.

Ross was laughing so hard he could barely talk. "That poor asshole. He clicked over and said, 'Hello?' And I said, 'For your information, Cliff, I wasn't dumped.' And then I hung up." We laughed insanely and maniacally for several minutes. This was the funniest thing I had ever heard of involving a telephone.

A few days later, during Algebra, I wrote a poem about it:

The wrath of God
Came down upon him,
As if to punish his hiding something.
Fire, brimstone
Bolts of lightning,
He really found the whole thing frightening.
Who could have known
Last Wednesday night,
That a cordless phone
Could ruin a life?

I copied it down and gave it to Ross for a little souvenir. It helped him get his mind off Tally.

The best conversations were with Joey. We talked every night and for a long, long time. He stood outside his family room on the back porch, pulling the phone cord as far as it would go. He leaned over the railing and tried to keep his voice down because his parents' window was just above him and they were always having to lean out and tell him to stop laughing so loudly, stop singing so loudly, stop clapping so loudly, stop talking so loudly, that he would wake the neighbors, that he was keeping *them* awake. I talked on the floor of my green room or in my green beanbag, the one that leaked beans because the cats liked to sit in it, too, or from the cave of my canopy bed.

We talked over the school day and about the weekend to come, but there was so much more. We discussed Our Lives Beyond School and what lay ahead for us. And the way we'd been Separated at Birth. We made up crazy stories, both literary and about the people we knew—we laughed about Tim Bullen chasing one of the fat Lawson twins (wearing wire sunglasses) on a beach, and the Seduction of Tommy Wissel (with his parents' reactions), and the Question of Black and White Love. We became enamored of Scott and Zelda Fitzgerald, convinced we were them reincarnate, and we wanted to leave as much for posterity and our biographers as they had. We began taping our conversations so that one day we would have a record:

Joey: "'The world is too much with us; late and soon . . .'"

Jennifer: "*This* world."

Joey: "What would our lives have been like if we'd been born some other place?"

Jennifer: "I *was* born some other place, but I still ended up here."

Joey: "What would our lives be like if we'd been raised some other place?"

Jennifer: "Like where? Los Angeles?" I was mad about Los Angeles.

Joey: "Anywhere." We are quiet as we imagine it.

Jennifer: "What if I'd never moved here at all? What if my parents had stayed in Maryland? What if you and I had never even met?" We are quiet again. As much as we hate Richmond, at least we are living through it together.

Joey: "I would still be best friends with Beverly Quigley. I would be talking to her right now. Probably about Jesus and *Remington Steele*."

Jennifer: "And I would be in Maryland, not quite as miserable, but lonelier because I wouldn't have you and Laura and Hether and Ross, but mostly you, although I like to think we would have found each other anyway."

Joey: "Or maybe we found each other here because here is where we need each other most?"

We are quiet for what is, for us, a long time (five seconds).

Joey: "If you were still in Maryland, you wouldn't know Tom Dehner."

(We begin talking very fast from this point on.)

Jennifer: "Oh my God, he looked so good today."

Joey: "He said hi to me at his locker. I was talking to Teresa and he said, 'What's up?'"

Jennifer: "How did he say it? Like, 'Hey, I really want to be your friend,' or literally 'What's up?'"

Joey: "Somewhere in between."

For the next hour we talk on and on about Tom Dehner.

When Joey's neighbors went on vacation, we walked over to their house and slipped in the back door and popped microwave popcorn while he made long-distance calls—to New York, to Los Angeles, to Paris, to Russia—not saying anything, just holding the line open so that even for a few minutes we could feel connected to another place, far, far outside of Richmond.

Academics

Through all the gripes and grumbles of what we hated about those pop quizzes, ten-minute speeches, and ten-page papers that were assigned, some good prevailed. What an accomplishment we felt when we finally finished that term paper we had worked on for nine weeks, or when we saw that "A" on the physics test we were sure we had flunked. We probably will never cease to be amazed that we actually did learn something in our time at school, even if it was to study in our assigned study halls or to know which stairs led up and which led down.

Kelley Robertson, Jo McQuiston, and Jennifer in math class

Algebra

What cares one for algebra?
Who delights in solving math?
I only want to live my life
Along the creative path.

—*Poem written by Jennifer in Algebra, 1985*

If I wanted to get help with math at home, the only option was my father. My mother was as hopeless at math as I was. My father, on the other hand, claimed to be good at it, but I never really knew if this was true because I did anything to avoid asking him for homework help, and this went for *any* subject. My dad had majored in history, and one of his great passions in life, next to humiliating me, running long distances, competing with me at almost everything, and cooking gourmet meals, was explaining things. If you asked him a simple question, like "Dad, could you please help me with my algebra?" he would say, "To fully understand algebra, we have to first go back to the beginning of time, to the year 21,000 B.C., before math was ever invented . . ." And then he would talk on and on and on, leading you up through the years, the discovery of math and all of its branches, the biographies of the greatest mathematicians, and sometime, many days later, he would get around to looking at the actual problem in the actual math book.

Instead, I asked our dog Tosh, my seventh-grade neighbor, the FedEx man, Joey (who was worse at math than I was), and even my mother before I asked my dad for help. Mom and I labored quietly, secretly, in my room, whispering so my dad wouldn't hear, trying between us to make one good math brain. We particularly hated story problems.

Mr. Brumley was a fat little man who looked just like a garden gnome, only without the red hat and suspenders. Each day before Algebra class, he stood in the hall, just outside his door, hands clasped behind his back. Sometimes, every now and then, he held them clasped in front of him. He nodded at students and watched them and yelled at them to slow down if they were running or walking too fast. "Exercise caution, Miss Ripperger!" "Walk, do not run, Mr. Wissel!"

Joey and I always seemed to end up in the same math classes together, but this was not true of Mr. Brumley's class. We both had him for Algebra second semester of our junior year, but Joey had him second period, and I had him fifth.

On one memorable day, Hether Rielly and I arrived at Mr. Brumley's classroom and he was standing in the hallway, his face a very bright red. His white hair looked more like smoke than hair. He didn't even nod at us as we walked in, just grumbled to himself, which was not like him at all.

"What's wrong with Mr. Brumley?" I said.

"Who knows?" said Hether. "The mysteries of the very old."

We sat down, waiting for the first bell to ring, and started asking around to see if anyone had done the homework. As usual, no one had. As a group, we then did what we usually did: we tried to get Rob Jarrett to give us the homework answers. Rob Jarrett and Tamela Vance were boyfriend and girlfriend. They weren't the most interesting people at parties, but they were both miraculously smart at math. Tamela Vance was in Joey's class, and everyone in there tried to copy off her. We, in turn, tried to copy off Rob. You couldn't always rely on them, though, because they fought a lot.

When Rob just sat there, not speaking, his math book closed, his notebooks on the floor by his feet, Hether said, "Great. What the hell are we supposed to do?"

Ross said, "Maybe you should do your homework, Hether," even though he never did his once the entire time I knew him.

Hether said, "Shut up, Ross."

The bell rang and Mr. Brumley walked into the room. He stood behind his desk and folded his hands, his face still a bright, dangerous red. He said, "Someone has taken the answer pages from my book, so we won't be able to go over the homework today. Let's move ahead with tomorrow's lesson." He opened his desk drawer, pulled out a piece of chalk, and began to write things on the board.

We all looked at one another. It was an outright miracle, too good to be believed. Rob Jarrett sat there, glaring at

Ross's back. He was the only one who seemed oblivious to the news.

Later that night, Joey told me what happened:

During second hour, Mr. Brumley stood in the hallway before the bell rang. No one had done the homework. Tamela sat in the back of the room sniffling and patting her eyes with a Kleenex. Panic ensued.

Deanna Haskett kept saying, "What are we going to do? What are we going to do?"

From his seat, Joey peered into the hallway. Mr. Brumley still stood there, hands clasped, alternately nodding and barking at students. Joey turned to Diane Armiger and said, "Keep them distracted." He meant Martha Schunk, who was so dutiful and self-righteous that she seemed more like an adult than one of us, and Deanna Haskett, who was a blabbermouth.

Diane complimented Martha on her penny loafers and then asked Deanna if she didn't have some just like them while Joey stood up and walked toward the front of the room. He marched right up to Mr. Brumley's desk and with one swift motion, ripped the homework pages from the book that lay open there. Joey carried the pages to the window, opened it, and flung them outside. He walked back to his seat and sat down.

Deanna Haskett, who had seen the whole thing, started saying, "OhmyGodohmyGodohmyGod!"

"What's she carrying on about?" Lance Powell said. Lance, who played on the basketball team, was so tall that he always sat at the back of the room because no one could see over his head. He took naps before class and sometimes during.

"Nothing!" Diane said.

The bell rang and Mr. Brumley appeared, shutting the door behind him. He marched over to his desk like a fat little general, hands still clasped, and said, "Let's go over the homework."

They all opened their books and their notebooks and sat there, waiting. Mr. Brumley circled around behind his desk, and picked up a piece of chalk. "Now." He glanced at his book. He peered closer at his book. He leaned forward and began flipping through pages. All the while, the top of his head, which was nearly hairless, was growing redder and redder. "Where have the pages gone?" he said. He kept flipping forward and backward through the book.

Everyone sat still as could be, even Deanna.

"Where are the pages?" He looked at them. "Who. Ripped. Out. These. Homework. Pages."

Deanna Haskett turned just slightly to look at Joey. Her eyes, already so far apart that they were practically on opposite sides of her head, were wide. Everyone looked around at one another innocently. Joey, with his blond choirboy haircut and glasses, looked the most innocent of all.

"Without these pages, we can't go over the homework," Mr. Brumley said.

Lance Powell, who had been dozing off again, raised his head and said, "What happened? Someone ripped a page out?"

"Lance Powell said he ripped the pages out?" Joey said, very low, looking all around, wide-eyed.

Tamela Vance stopped sniffling long enough to say, loud enough for everyone to hear, "Lance ripped the pages out?"

Mr. Brumley stopped what he was doing. He turned and stared at the back of the room. "Lance Powell, did you rip these pages out?"

Lance sat up and rubbed his eyes. "No."

Mr. Brumley glared at him. "I'm not going to ask you again."

Lance said, "I didn't rip the pages."

Mr. Brumley stared at Lance for a good, long minute. Then he picked up a piece of chalk and his textbook and said, "I hope whoever did this is happy. Because of you we can't learn the math for today. You may never learn the math we were supposed to learn today. That may be your one and only chance in this world. And someone has ruined it for you. We'll just have to go on to tomorrow's lesson."

Toward the end of the semester in Mr. Brumley's class, on a particular day in May, the school year was winding down, and the second floor was hot, and I was full and sleepy from lunch, and the idea of one more math class was almost too much to bear. Hether and I walked to class together from Humanities and she said, "I hate math."

I said, "I hate math, too."

Lori Bechtel was walking behind us, on her way to Mr. Brumley's class. "I hate it, too," she said.

"Let's ditch," Hether said.

We can't do that, I thought. I was always afraid of getting in trouble. I blamed this on my mother, who, I was sure, had never done anything naughty in her life. I had heard story after story at my grandmother's house about my aunt Lynn getting caught smoking, or my uncle Bill smuggling a goat into a classroom, or my aunt Doris putting Elmer's Glue on the teacher's chair. But no one ever said anything about my mom except that she was the valedictorian and a majorette and president of the student council and Miss Hi Miss and a cheerleader, plus the organist at the Methodist church.

Out loud, I said, "Okay." Immediately my heart started racing. Ditching was not something I usually did, even though I had friends, namely Tommy Wissel, who did it all the time.

Lori and Hether and I were already near Mr. Brumley's classroom. He was standing outside, hands folded, and we turned around before he could see us and walked the other way, straight into Ross.

"Class is that way," he said, turning me around and pointing me in the right direction. He began pushing me along like a wheelbarrow.

Hether was jumping at him like a little yappy dog. "Let her go, Ross, you big Jew!" She and Lori, who was tall and sturdy and played on the tennis team, pulled him off me.

"I've got cramps, Ross," I said. "I'm going to the nurse."

"Me too," said Lori.

"Me too," said Hether.

Ross snorted and walked away backward. "My big white Jewish ass!" he yelled.

We made a right and slipped down the stairs toward the cafeteria. We hid in the concession area, which was behind a stone wall painted red. When the bell rang, we leaned against the Coke machine.

"Where should we go?" I asked. I was nervous because Mr. Lebo, the dean of students, had a way of being everywhere at once.

"We could stay here," Lori said.

"No," said Hether. "We need to keep moving. If anyone stops us, just say that we have cramps and are going to the nurse."

We heard the rapid tap-tapping of heels going past. They paused and then tapped toward the cafeteria.

"Come on," Hether said.

We moved together through the halls of the school, which were deserted. They looked strange and hollow. The floors were shiny. The lockers scuffed. These were things I never had time to notice when 2,500 students were pushing and fighting their way to class.

We headed down the Smokers Hall, past the swimming pool. The air smelled stale and sweet, like cigarettes and chlorine. We crept under the windows of the athletic offices and then stopped cold when we got to the basketball court, where Mr. Fleagle was teaching a freshman P.E. class. We backed up and went around the other way, up the end of the hallway by my AP History class, and toward Social Hall. Because Social Hall sprawled outside the principal's office, we slipped up the stairs to the second floor.

We walked quickly. Where was Mr. Lebo? Our goal was the art museum. We thought if we could get there we'd be safe because we might be mistaken for art-loving tourists, out for an afternoon's sightseeing excursion. Suddenly Mr. Wysong appeared and we sprinted back down the stairs. We backtracked then, past my AP History room, back toward the Tiernan Center, back by the swimming pool, and up through Smokers Hall.

"Let's go to the cafeteria," said Lori.

We headed back that way, but there was a sudden tap-tapping of heels again, which sent us scurrying up the steps to the second floor. The long hallway was clear, but the tricky thing now was that we had to walk by Mr. Brumley's classroom. His door was closed, but there was a window in the door, and we didn't want to risk being seen.

"What do we do now?" Lori said. We looked at one another, hovering at the end of the hallway, near the top of the stairs. It was always dark down there, like the janitor just couldn't be bothered to change the bulbs in the ceiling. It gave me the creeps. It looked like the exact spot in school where something mean and scary would happen if we were starring in a horror movie and not our real lives. I wished we'd gone to class. I was starting to get a very bad feeling.

"We just walk by as fast as we can," Hether said. "And if anyone stops us, we say we're headed to the nurse."

We set out together, all in a line, walking very quickly, heads down. As we passed Mr. Brumley's room, I glanced back and saw Ross's face.

"There they go!" he shouted. "Jennifer, Hether, and Lori are out there, Mr. Brumley!" Mr. Brumley threw open the door and we ran.

"We have cramps!" I yelled. We all clutched our stomachs.

There was the pattering of little feet as Mr. Brumley sprinted after the three of us. *Dear God, what have I done?* I thought. Instead of cutting down the middle stairs to the central hallway and, eventually, the nurse's office, we ran like track stars down the second-floor hall. At the end of the hall, we turned right and raced up the stairs to the third floor, taking them three at a time. Mr. Brumley came puffing along behind us.

We ran back down, back to the second floor, toward the Tiernan Center. We could hear his feet on the shiny floors. We skidded up the handicap ramp, past the offices of the gym teachers and coaches, through the doors to the pool, down through the Smokers Hall.

"Do you see him?" screamed Lori.

"Keep running!" Hether yelled.

We rounded the corner into the main hallway and

sprinted for the nurse's office. We were sitting down when Mr. Brumley burst in, one minute later, face purple. Unable to speak, he pointed at us.

Lori was doubled over in her chair, trying to breathe. "Lori was sick, Mr. Brumley," I said. "Hether and I got so scared. We were in the bathroom and she just fell over and said she had cramps. We had to get her down here as fast as we could."

His face wrinkled up and he finally managed words. "You girls." *Puff puff.* He waved at Hether and me. "Just come on up," *puff puff,* "when you're done." *Puff puff.* "And, Miss Bechtel, I hope you feel better soon."

He waddled out, wiping his brow with the handkerchief he kept in his front shirt pocket. We looked at one another. "I feel so bad now," I said.

"Me too," said Lori. "We could have given him a heart attack."

"I don't," said Hether. "We got out of math class, didn't we?"

We spent the rest of the period reading magazines and talking to the nurse, who gave us Tylenol for our cramps and then wrote us a note excusing us from next period, too.

handle ourselves in case Richmond was attacked by nuclear weapons.

They showed *The Day After* to us in two parts since it was too long for a single class period. I was sleepless for weeks. It was bad enough to imagine a nuclear war, but thinking about surviving it—limbs falling off, flesh melting, all those blind people at the end. Nuclear devastation was the most horrible, frightening thing I could imagine. I was sure the Russians were going to bomb us and I was going to die a miserable, wretched death just like the people on screen.

In my bright green room, surrounded by my posters— the Stray Cats, Duran Duran, Bono, the Police, Bob Geldof, Fleetwood Mac, Rick Springfield—I lay on my yellow canopy bed and imagined a world without my mother or father, my dog or my cat, my best friends, the boys I liked, the music I listened to, the things I dreamed of, much less trees or houses or grass or arms. I moved my head and my legs around. I felt the skin on my hands, my face. I made myself think fast about the world I lived in—one where people were neighborly to one another and spelled out "It's Spring!" in tulips on the grounds of Glen Miller Park and took pictures of goats and didn't do much but steal from one another every now and then, but only small things and not very often.

Jennifer's mom at her office typewriter

Typing

The pen is mightier than the sword, but a well-aimed type-writer packs a good punch, too.

—*Anonymous*

It was my mom's idea that I take Typing. Before she suggested it, Typing was just one of the many classes I was vaguely aware of that existed in the new Career Center just off the cafeteria. Everything over there smelled shiny and clean and fresh and cool and looked like something made by Mattel. Ivy Tech Community College shared the facilities with us and there were wildly exotic-sounding classes like Vocational and Industrial Arts Management, which included Auto Mechanics, Machine Shop, Building Trades, Home Economics, and Agriculture. There were also secretarial classes and computer classes, although I wouldn't have been caught dead in a computer class. Computers were something only the strangest of strange boys studied—the nerdiest of nerds, the brainiacs. Boys who wore ties and didn't wash their hair and always, always got the labs right in Chemistry.

My mother typed all the time because she was working on a book—the first official biography in all the world of the poet Carl Sandburg—and my mom said she couldn't possibly write it without knowing how to type. I had always handwritten my own songs and stories—stories about the Vietnam War and prisons and mysteries and horses, and, best of all, stories about Jennifer Niven, world-famous rock star, who travels from country to country with her younger and very sexy boyfriend. But I thought maybe typing would save me time and allow me to write faster. If I wrote faster, I could turn out more stories.

I decided to get Typing out of the way as soon as possible and signed up for it first semester sophomore year. The typewriters sat on our desks—enormous blocks—so huge you could barely see over them or past them. They were impossible to pick up, so God forbid you had to move them for any reason. We sat alphabetically. School was still new and we were still new to it and one another. There was a cute boy behind me with blond hair and glasses. He was lanky and had a nice smile. He slouched in his chair, which made him immediately seem cooler than anyone else.

When Mrs. Young called role the first day she said, "Jennifer McJunkin?"

I said, "Here."

Then she said, "Ned Mitchell?"

The slouchy boy behind me mumbled, "Here."

I sat there thinking, *Ned Mitchell. Ned Mitchell.* It was a name that was very familiar. And then it hit me with visions of monkey bars and jungle gyms and cracked gray asphalt and foursquare lines on pavement. I hadn't seen Ned Mitchell since fourth grade when we played *Charlie's Angels* at Westview Elementary, when he was Charlie, sitting in the middle of the domed jungle gym, passing out undercover assignments to Heather Craig, Susie Leggett, and me. He was one of my first best friends in Richmond, until he moved away to another part of town, another school district. It was like he'd vanished from the earth. And now all these years later, there he was behind me.

I turned in my seat and said, "Charlie? Charlie Townsend, is that you?"

He blinked at me for a minute, scrunching down in his chair, too lazy and cool to sit like a normal person. Then he said, "What?"

I said, "It's me. Kelly Garrett. Your angel."

He stared at me like I was insane. And then, suddenly, a light came into his eyes and swept over his face and he sat up just a little. "Good morning, Angel," he said.

From that moment on, we were best friends again. We exchanged phone numbers and talked every night on the telephone, long into the wee hours, even after I was supposed to be asleep. After my mom told me good night and I turned off my light, I'd dial Ned back and lie there under the covers talking to him. We could talk about anything in the world.

Sometimes Ned would call me from the bathtub, where I tried not to picture his naked feet, which for some reason bothered me more than the rest of him being naked and soapy. He knew his feet bothered me, so he always mentioned them. Like, "Guess what I'm doing with my feet right now? I'm clogging up the drain spout with my big toe."

I told him I would hang up on him if he kept talking like that.

"I think you can tell a lot about a person by his feet," Ned said one night.

"I don't like feet," I said.

"Any feet?"

"I like my feet."

"But no one else's?"

I thought about this. "I like my cat's feet."

"People feet."

"No."

"Why yours and only yours?"

"I have pretty toes." I was lying on my yellow bed. I held my feet up then and waved them around so that the nail polish sparkled. On the other end of the line Ned splashed around. I tried not to hear the water.

He said, "What do you think Mr. Lebo's feet look like?"

"Don't." I pushed the pillow around my ears.

"I bet they have hairs on them and long yellow toenails."

"I'm going to hang up the phone."

"Like a hobbit."

I was suffocating myself with the pillow.

"What about Mr. Fleagle's feet?" Mr. Fleagle was my Driver's Ed teacher. I thought about him pushing on the emergency brake over and over again while I drove. "I bet they're long and scaly like a rat."

"Oh my God." I couldn't stand it. I had the pillow over my head.

"What about Mrs. Young's feet?"

. "She might have pretty feet," I said through the pillow.

"Maybe." I could hear the water splashing. "Tom Mangas has ugly feet." Tom was Ned's best friend, but they were always competing over everything.

I didn't say anything to this because it was probably true.

And then, for the next two hours, we went through the entire faculty and student body—everyone from Principal Denney French to Tom Dehner—guessing what their feet looked like.

One night, Ned and I had been on the phone for an especially long time. The cord to my green phone (which perfectly matched the walls of my room) was knotted and twisted from all my pacing. The cord was so long that to unwind it I had to stand on top of a chair or, better yet, my desk, which was a sturdy old sewing table that no longer had the sewing machine but did have the foot pedal, which I loved to push-push-push while I worked or read or wrote. On this particular night, Ned and I had been talking for at least three hours without a break.

Around nine, I heard my father come home. I couldn't hear exactly what he was saying, but his voice was loud and I could tell he was unhappy. A few minutes later, there was a knock on my door. "Jennifer?" It was my mom. She opened the door and poked her head in. "Your father has been trying to call for three hours."

My stomach did a little flip. "Oh?"

"Ned?"

"Uh-huh."

"Well, why don't you tell him good night."

After she had gone, I told Ned what had happened and that I was being made to go, and we grumbled about the unfairness of it all.

The next day, my father called the phone company and ordered call-waiting. This was a very big deal because most people didn't have call-waiting. For months, my mom and I had been telling him we needed it but he kept saying it was a waste of money.

My parents sat me down in the living room.

"This does not mean you can talk for hours on the phone, just because people can now get through," my dad said. "We did not have this installed so that you could talk indefinitely."

"Of course."

"It also doesn't mean that you can talk to one person on one line and another person on another line and go back and forth between them."

"Okay." I had never even thought of this. *Call-waiting is a miracle. The possibilities are endless.*

"Do you understand?"

"Yes."

I couldn't wait to call Ned to tell him about the call-waiting. I figured now we could talk on the phone all night if we wanted to.

We were in danger of failing Typing. Not just because we stayed up half the night talking, which meant we were seriously sleep deprived, but because we typed each other notes in class when we were supposed to be typing things like: *The little duck swims in the pond as the sun settles in the sky.* Mrs. Young, so patient, so kind, threatened to separate us if we didn't straighten up.

Then there came a magical day when the sun was out and my hair actually looked good and Tom Mangas wrote me a note in Spanish class, asking me out to a movie for that coming weekend. My heart was light and free and the very next period I would see Ned and we would type notes to each other about people's feet and try not to laugh too hard so that we didn't get in trouble, and that night we would talk for hours, and then there would be just three more days before the weekend and my date.

I got to class before Ned and was just getting things set up for the hour when he came stalking into the room. He breezed by me and sat down behind me and ripped the cover off his typewriter and threw it onto the floor and started pounding on the keys. I turned around and said, "What's wrong?"

He glanced up, just once, and gave me a sort of death stare.

I said, "What?"

He said, "I hear you're going out with Mangas."

I thought, *Wow, news travels fast.* But out loud I said, "That's right." His fingers went *bang-bang-bang* on the keys. I said, "You're going to break the typewriter if you keep doing that."

He said, "Why don't you turn around and do your work?"

For almost thirty seconds I couldn't speak. I just stared at him. I said, "What is wrong with you?"

He said, "Nothing. What's wrong with you?"

Mrs. Young said, "Jennifer, Ned, class has started. Please keep it down. Jennifer, turn around please."

Ned smiled to himself, a gloaty, mean sort of smile. His fingers went *bang-bang-bang.* I turned around and lifted the cover off my typewriter and folded it up and set it on top of my books. I got out a piece of blank paper and slipped it into the carriage and opened my typing book and began to copy the day's lesson.

The red rooster runs around the barnyard twenty times . . .

Everyone else went *clickety-clack*, *clickety-clickety* on the keys, but Ned sat there going *bang-bang-bang* in my ear. I knew the entire time he was typing at me. When the bell rang, he threw the cover back onto the typewriter and grabbed his books and pushed past me before I could even stand up. He didn't call me that night. Or the night after. Or the night after. He stopped talking to me completely. Every day it was the same—*bang-bang-bang. Bang-bang-bang.*

Mrs. Young would say, "Ned, please type a little softer. You're going to break the machine."

Bang-bang-bang.

I didn't say a word to him. I wasn't about to give him the satisfaction. Instead I came into class and sat down at my desk and stared at my typewriter or straight ahead and learned exactly what I was supposed to learn. I paid attention. I didn't talk or write notes. That weekend, I went out with Tom Mangas. I said, "Has Ned said anything to you?"

He said, "No."

The rest of the semester it was the same. I stopped dating Tom and started dating Eric Lundquist, and Ned still wouldn't talk to me. But I got an A in Typing, and that Christmas, my parents bought me a typewriter—smaller than a car, smart and electric and fast. I set it up on my sewing table desk underneath my window and wrote story after story, poems and songs and novellas about life beyond Richmond.

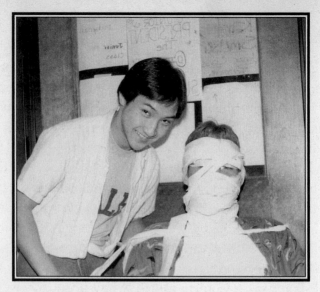

Robert Ignacio and Ned Mitchell in Health class

Our Good Health and Safety

This hour isn't just a class—it's an adventure. Students may be introduced to shuffleboard, archery, and crab-soccer. They also have the chance to skate, but are not required to. Along with fun there has to be safety. One of the big-time happenings in this class is learning CPR. And bandaging each other is really more fun than study.

— *1984* Pierian

When we first moved to Richmond, one of our neighbors tried to make friends with my mother. Mrs. Harper belonged to several bowling leagues and teams and was always inviting my mom to bowl. My mom was not a bowler and would come up with polite excuses as to why she could never join her. Until one day, when Mrs. Harper asked again, and Mom said no again—she was working on her book; she and my dad were hosting a party for his work; she was helping me with a school project; she had to clean the house.

When my mom was done talking, Mrs. Harper shook her head and looked at my mother with a great deal of pity. She said, "You poor thing. You must never get to bowl."

The summer before my junior year, I took summer school gym because the session was shorter and we did things like play tennis, which I was at least decent at, and which they didn't do during the regular school year. I signed up for classes with Joey.

When it came time for the bowling part of class, we piled onto a school bus and drove to the east side of town, past the mall, to 40 Lanes, which had a pro shop, an arcade, a snack bar, a nursery, and a lounge. I wasn't one bit interested in bowling. I hated the ugly shoes and the stale smell of the place—a combination of socks and old feet and cigarettes and beer. Tennis was one thing. I was good at tennis. Bowling was another. I had never bowled. I might not be good at it, and I didn't like to not be good at things. When it was my turn to bowl, I said, "I don't care if I never bowl in my life. Who wants to bowl for me?"

Joey was the fastest to volunteer. He grabbed a ball and jammed his fingers inside and went marching toward the pins. He said, "I hope you're watching this. Because this is how it's done." He flung his arm back and let the ball go and at the same time he went flying forward onto his stomach and slid halfway down the lane. Just like in a movie. The ball went right into the gutter. We all clapped and cheered. He did this over and over again. In the end, my total score was a nine and I hadn't once picked up a ball.

On the bus ride home, Mr. Fleagle came barreling down the aisle, his face red, and shouted: "Where's McJunkin?"

I was sitting next to Joey, laughing and talking. I said, "Here."

He shouted, "A *NINE?!*"

I just blinked at him and shrugged. I didn't think it was a good idea to mention that I hadn't done my own bowling. I said, "I don't seem to be cut out for this sport."

He stared at me. I hadn't seen him this furious since Driver's Ed. He said, "You can say that again!" He went back down the aisle, back to the front of the bus, sputtering and muttering, shaking his head, talking to himself.

After the summer of 1984, I never bowled again.

During our sophomore year, we were forced to take Health. This was where we learned CPR and practiced bandaging each other, which meant we turned ourselves into mummies when our teacher, Mr. Rogers, wasn't looking.

Mr. Rogers was very serious. He knew that he had been entrusted with a great responsibility, that he was teaching us perhaps the most important lessons we would ever learn in our lives. Because of this, he tried not to lose his temper when we used up all the bandaging tape on our mummification rituals and went stumbling into walls, blinded and sightless, our arms stretched out before us. Time and again, he tried to impress upon us the seriousness of life. He made it very clear that our homes were "accidents waiting to happen."

I was already paranoid about driving, thanks to Mr. Kemper and Mr. Fleagle, and now I became nervous in my own house. Everywhere I looked, I wondered if things were going to catch fire or explode without warning (for some reason, these were the accidents that came to mind). I made my mother buy extra fire extinguishers and test the smoke alarms. My parents bought a rope ladder we could use to climb out of the second-floor windows if we ever had to. We went over an emergency evacuation plan, in case we had to leave the house quickly—who would be responsible for grabbing the cat, the dog, my ABBA albums, my best shoes, my hair spray, etc.

One day Mr. Rogers announced that we were having an all-school assembly so that we could watch a film on the dangers of doing drugs. This was exciting, of course, because it meant getting out of class. It was early in our sophomore year, when we were still new to the school. Mr. Rogers lined us up and we followed him down to Civic Hall, where the entire school was gathered.

Principal French stood on the stage with a giant movie screen behind him. He tested the microphone and it squeaked and squawked, making us groan and cover our ears. He said, "Sorry, sorry. Some of our friends have joined us today from the Richmond Police Department." He waved at a group of officers who sat in the front row on the floor of the gym. "They've been kind enough to bring a film to share with you about a very real problem, and afterward they will be on hand to answer any questions you might have. I thought this was a very important thing for all of us to learn about because drugs are terrible and such a problem not only in this country but in this school. There is drug use going on right this very minute around us, and maybe this will help put a stop to it."

I looked around me and wondered who was doing drugs right this minute. I didn't see anyone doing anything unusual, but then I didn't know anything about drugs, other than what I'd read in *Rolling Stone* and the one book I owned about Donovan and the Beatles.

The film started and it wasn't animated but real—with real people (played by actors) and real situations. There were a lot of needles. There were kids shooting needles into their arms at school and in parks and at home. Anywhere they could shoot up, they were shooting up with those needles. They shot up in cars and in alleyways and at movie theaters. And then they threw up and walked into walls and yelled at their parents and made them cry, and then they found some more needles and shot up again. I thought it seemed unrealistic, and the acting was really bad—worse than on *Fantasy Island*.

After a long time of all this shooting up, the kids who were doing it were then rushed to the emergency room and then there were more needles as the doctors and nurses were sticking needles in their arms to give them IVs. I had seen *Trapper John, M.D.* and I didn't think this was realistic at all. There had never been a single episode in which so many kids were rushed to the hospital at once for using drugs.

But the strangest thing was happening around me. Everywhere I looked, people were falling over in and out of their seats. Every now and then someone stood up and wobbled and a teacher ran forward and caught them. It was mostly girls. A few of them were crying. Students were sway-ing back and forth and teachers were running this way and that, trying to keep them from falling over. Some of them were so overcome by the movie, they just fainted outright.

Across the auditorium, upstairs near the front of the screen, Joey stood up from where he was sitting with his World History classmates. He started down the long concrete steps that led to the next level, down to the floor, and that's when I saw him, teetering there, before a teacher caught him and handed him to Lance Powell, who led him out of Civic Hall.

He could have died falling down those stairs, I thought.

When the lights went on, we got up and filed out with our classes. I felt a little shaky. The room had gotten hotter and hotter. So many students were missing. Later I learned they had been taken to a room—all girls, Steve Kutter, who was a hood, and Joey.

When Joey recovered the ability to speak he said to Steve, "Man, that was some film, huh?"

Steve said, "Shut up!" He walked to the other side of the room and faced the wall, too embarrassed to even look at Joey. He didn't talk to him again for a week.

As I walked out of Civic Hall I thought, *However bad drugs are, they can't be as bad as what we saw in that movie.* Drug films were every bit as dangerous as drugs themselves.

Jennifer and Joey

Teachers

Everyone looks particularly tired and Midwestern across the room today.

—Joey to Jennifer in Mrs. Thompson's Russian Lit. class

Mrs. Thompson taught my favorite class of all time, Russian Literature. It was very popular and everyone took it at one time or another even if they hated English or reading or school or Russia (which a lot of people did at that time because we were so afraid of nuclear war).

Mrs. Thompson was petite but had enormous black hair that seemed almost suspended above her head. Her husband worked at Earlham with my father.

Joey and I took Russian Literature together. My girlfriends Hether Rielly, Hillary Moretti, and Diane Armiger were also in there, along with Gina Hurd (whose brightly patterned outfits we loved to make fun of) and Sean Mayberry, who was so big and strong and gorgeous it was hard to know where to look. Sean was good friends with Tom Dehner, and I sometimes caught him looking at me, which was, I thought, the next best thing to being flirted with by Tom Dehner himself.

I was wild about Russian Literature. I loved the books and the writers—especially Turgenev's *Fathers and Sons* and Dostoevsky's *Brothers Karamazov*. I read every book Mrs. Thompson assigned us, and I never used CliffsNotes like most of my friends. Joey and I both did well on our papers and participated in class, and something about all that excitement made us especially prolific when it came to our note writing. We sat next to each other and not only passed notes, but after a while we carried on entire conversations in our spiral notebooks. Not about the class, of course, but about the people in it (usually Sean Mayberry and his intentions toward me, or Gina Hurd and her crazy wardrobe) and about Mrs. Thompson, and about all the other many, many things in the world that interested us. The paper never left our notebooks—we just each wrote down our side of the dialogue on our own pages and looked over now and then to read what the other had to say. Through it all, we were very quiet. We didn't speak a word. Unfortunately, Mrs. Thompson wasn't stupid. She watched Joey and me like hawks.

Every so often she separated us, placing me on the opposite side of the room by Diane, who had chosen to separate herself from Joey, Hether, Hill, and me because she said we distracted her too much, and she would never get anything done sitting beside us. When she saw me coming, she did a bit of eye rolling. Now, because we sat in a kind of half circle, I was directly across from Joey, which meant we could mouth things to each other. Every time Mrs. Thompson would turn to the board, Joey would mime something and I would mime something back. Sometimes Joey would write something down in his notebook, big enough for me to read, and hold it up. The unfortunate thing was that everyone else could read it, too.

I still remembered some sign language from sixth grade—from the time Heather Craig and I learned it so we could communicate across the room—so after school one day I taught some to Joey. Unfortunately, I had only taught myself the individual letters of the alphabet, so it was very slow having to spell out words, much less entire sentences, one letter at a time. Joey and I tried this the next day in class, but it took too long to spell things, and Mrs. Thompson kept turning around, which made us have to start over again. Every time she turned around, she'd look at us, first Joey, then me, and she'd frown.

Finally, after a week of this, she let us sit together again, but she gave us a warning. She said, "My eyes are on you." She looked mostly at Joey as she said it. "I know you are good friends. You are two of my best students, but don't let me catch you talking to each other anymore during this class."

I decided it was best not to point out that, technically, we weren't actually *talking*, because I had learned my lesson about that back in seventh grade after an unfortunate run-in with my sewing teacher. Instead, we promised Mrs. Thompson and nodded and said we would be good. The next day, I opened my notebook and started copying down Mrs. Thompson's lecture dutifully. To the left of me, Joey made a little noise. I ignored him. He made it again. I looked over out of the corner of my eye. On his paper, he had written, *Gina is looking especially lovely today.*

And we were off and running.

Joey and I were, as a rule, competitive with each other—in speech meets and in English classes. I wouldn't cheat for him on quizzes, much as he asked me to, and he sometimes beat me at grades and I sometimes beat him. Somehow we almost always came out even. But on one memorable day, Mrs. Thompson gave Joey an extension on some work, which I thought was unfair.

Teacher's pet, I wrote to him. *She loooooooves you.*

He wrote back, *Oh, calm down. It's a one-day extension. Not a proposal of marriage.*

I wrote, *A one-day extension that no one else got, Mr. Sensitive. Did I hit a nerve?*

He wrote, *Um. No. But you've certainly got nerve.*

Suddenly we were fighting. This had never happened before. We sat side by side, not writing back and forth. I didn't hear a word of Mrs. Thompson's lecture. Hether slipped me a note but I didn't even open it.

That night, Joey didn't call me and I didn't call him. My mom said, "The phone is awfully quiet." She picked it up to make sure it was working. I sighed at her and went up to bed early and didn't even turn on the television. I just got in my bed and lay there wondering if this was it, if the very best friendship I'd ever had was over. Suddenly I had visions of myself alone in Richmond without Joey, trying to survive RHS on my own till graduation, and it was terrifying. Of course I blamed him. He was too touchy, I told myself. It wasn't fair that he should get preferential treatment. Just lying there, I got mad all over again. I hadn't been this mad at him since he stole Tom Dehner's class schedule from the guidance office and managed to get changed into all his classes when I hadn't been able to change a single one of my own.

The next day, Joey and I sat in class not writing notes. Mrs. Thompson seemed relieved and happy. To be honest, she seemed elated. She smiled. She laughed. She practically skipped from her desk to the blackboard. The happier she was, the madder I got. Over and over, I glanced at Joey out of the corner of my eye, but he wouldn't look at me.

I went home that night and once again he didn't call me and I didn't call him. The next day I couldn't stand it— Mrs. Thompson skipping and smiling, uninterpreted glances from Sean Mayberry, a particularly outlandish outfit from Gina, and Joey sulking at me (he could sulk better than anyone I knew). I wrote him a note.

Since this is a week to say what we want, let's quit being children. Shall we? I'll apologize for teasing you, if you apologize for snapping my head off. Really, Gina is too good to waste today. Besides, the class is wondering why we're so quiet.

I passed the note to Joey. He wrote, *Well I don't really appreciate being forever told Mrs. Thompson is catering to me when she gave me a one-day extension one time. It's not like I'm working any less hard than anyone else. But it's a good thing we cleared this up because I need to say two things: 1st, how good Sean Mayberry looks across the room, and 2nd, where in the hell did Gina buy that outfit, the Circus Shoppe?*

We wrote back and forth for a bit, wondering if Gina got dressed in the dark, where Mrs. Thompson had her hair styled, what Sean Mayberry was thinking when he smiled at me like that. Then, at one point, Mrs. Thompson turned around from the board in midsentence and froze. She was looking directly at us. We weren't doing anything that she could see. Joey was writing on his paper. I was writing on mine. We were being the epitome of subtlety. But we were smiling in a very familiar way. All the color seemed to leave her cheeks. She stopped speaking. Slowly she turned back to the board, and, after a moment, began writing again.

Joey wrote: *Poor Mrs. T. For a while she thought we were finally split up.*

I wrote back, *It will take a lot more than Russian Literature to tear us apart.*

Jennifer and Joey at the Carl Sandburg House in North Carolina

How I Spent My Summer

I just want to go far, far away from here—some place where they've never heard of Indiana.

—Jennifer to Joey, 1985

My friends liked to come over to my house to get a little culture. My parents did things that many of my friends' parents didn't do. My mother played the piano. My father smoked a pipe. My father drove a classic old Jaguar with real leather seats, and later a Mercedes. My dad ran marathons in faraway places like Boston and New York City. My mother wrote books. My parents had both been to college and even to graduate school. They spoke foreign languages. Our walls were painted bright colors, not just white or off-white. My parents collected Japanese art and Persian rugs and had once lived in Asia. My dad could speak Hindi and Urdu. My mom still remembered some of the Okinawan dances she had learned when we were living there. We were Quakers. My father was a gourmet chef in his spare time. My parents had wine with dinner. And during spring break and in the summers, we traveled.

All of these things gave us an air of fascination to my friends, most of whose parents had been born and raised in Richmond, and hadn't been to college, and worked sensible jobs, and came home to sensible houses with white walls and art that had been purchased at Hackman-Eickemeyer Furniture or Bullerdick Furniture or Target or Webb's Antique Mall in Centerville. They ate casseroles for dinner and during summer they drove to Indianapolis or Dayton or Brookville Lake, or just stayed home.

In the ninth grade, I competed on a history team with some of my classmates. We won the regional and state rounds of competition, which meant we traveled to Washington, D.C., to compete in nationals. My parents chaperoned us and, when we weren't performing, they took us to see the sights since they were familiar with the city.

When we got home to Indiana, Ruthie Mullen wrote my parents a thank-you note: *Visiting Washington with you was very interesting and definitely a terrific experience. I now want to become a balloonist, a first lady, an astronaut, an architect, and, of course, a historian with a foreign accent.* My parents helped open the world to my friends.

I first went to New York with my parents in June of 1982. Rick Springfield, whose posters covered my walls, was playing at Carnegie Hall. When they told us at the box office that tickets were sold out, that they'd been sold out for weeks, my father spent an hour talking to scalpers until he found the very best seats. The only catch was that he could only get two tickets together (or so he said). He and my mother argued over who would take me.

"You should go with her," my dad said. "She'll have more fun with you."

"No," my mom said. "You bought her the tickets. You should go. I insist."

"I wouldn't hear of it. You go."

"No, no. You."

Back and forth, back and forth, politely but firmly arguing because neither one of them wanted to go to the Rick Springfield concert. In the end, my mom lost, and my dad walked us there and dropped us off and then practically ran for the nearest deli, happy to be free of the mob scene of chattering teen and preteen girls and their mothers. My mom spent the entire concert in the lobby with the other mothers, Kleenex stuffed into her ears, while all the girls but me screamed and cried over Rick and I tried hard to hear him over all the noise. It was my first rock concert.

We went back to New York after that for visits here and there, and in the summer of 1985, while my dad stayed in Richmond, too busy to join us, my mom and I lived for almost a month in the city while she organized the papers of playwright Horton Foote. We stayed in Horton's apartment in Greenwich Village and sorted through boxes of letters and old manuscripts and finished and unfinished scripts.

Joey came to visit and stayed for a week. Joey's mom had been born at Reid Hospital in Richmond. She graduated from Richmond High School in 1964. Mike Kraemer came from Wisconsin, but he had lived in Richmond for thirty years and never planned to live anywhere else. This

was Joey's first time in New York and he fell in love with it
instantly. We sat on the floor of Horton's office and held
the Oscars he won for *Tender Mercies* and *To Kill a Mock-
ingbird*. We pretended they were ours and took turns posing
for pictures with them. Then we stretched out on the floor,
side by side, and looked through the family albums because
we knew that Horton's daughter Daisy Foote, which was
one of the funniest names we had ever heard, was dating at
that time a boy we were very much in love with: Matthew
Broderick. We wanted to take all the pictures he was in for
ourselves and slip them into our own photo albums, or take
them back to school with us and show them to our friends
or to the girls who were mean to me to show them how cool
we were in our real lives outside of Richmond High School.

My mom took us to Broadway shows, to Lincoln Center, to the ballet, to museums, and to Sunday brunch at the
Waldorf. We sat on the hood of a cab at the U.N. and posed
for pictures, and did Bloomingdale's, and Trump Tower, but
the highlight was seeing *Biloxi Blues* on Broadway. At one
point Matthew Broderick's character said, "I just want a girl
to say, 'Eugene, I'm here, come get me!'" and we burst into
a fit of giggles that made Matthew forget his next line. The
usher had to come down the aisle and ask us to be quiet, but
we wanted to stand up then and there and shout it back to
Matthew: "Eugene, we're here! Come get us!"

In the afternoons and evenings, Joey and I sat in the big
picture window in Horton's bedroom, three floors up from
the world, above the trees, legs dangling, and looked out
over the transvestites and young professionals and thugs—
all the humanity! We could see the lights of "Liberty" down
the river and the outline of the Twin Towers and the sound
of distant laughter from down below, from far away, from

over in New Jersey, and we talked about how our lives were just beginning, about all the things we would do, the places we would go. In the mornings, we walked down to the corner store and bought bagels for breakfast. Then we walked back and stood outside the apartment building and looked out at the river and the Statue of Liberty in the distance and talked of future times when we would be famous.

One day, on our way back to the apartment, we passed a patch of freshly poured cement at a construction site. Joey picked up a rock and wrote *Joe Kraemer*. Below it, I wrote *Jennifer Niven*, which was the name I wanted to use one day when I was an actress or a writer. Joey added an *and* in between our names, and below them he wrote *forever*.

At the end of the week, Joey went back to Richmond, and then it was just my mom and me. We worked in the apartment during the day, organizing Horton's papers. At night we slipped out into the city and went to see *A Chorus Line* or an off-Broadway play or met friends for dinner.

About a week after Joey left, my mother and I were fixing lunch, around twelve-thirty or so, when the telephone rang.

"Mom, would you get that?" I said, because I hated answering the phone there.

"No, my hands are full, you'll have to get it."

Oh God. Sigh. Complain. Complain. Groaning, I turned the TV volume down to low, and on the third ring, picked up the phone. "Horton Foote residence, Jennifer McJunkin speaking."

"Hi, is this the answering service?"

Not knowing what to say, I said, "Yes."

"Oh," the voice said. "Could I speak to Daisy, please?"

(Panic . . . momentary curiosity . . . a quiet, nagging thought in the back of my mind.)

"She's not here right now, could I take a message?"

(Pause.)

"Well, yes, could you tell her Matthew called?"

I KNEW IT!! I knew it! I knew it!

"Sure, would you like me to have her call you?" (How I got the words out and remained calm, I'll never know.)

"No, just tell her I called." (Pause.) "You know, this doesn't really sound like an answering service."

(Laughter from both as I said:)

"We're friends of the family and we're staying in the apartment."

"Oh . . . then Daisy definitely isn't there. You checked under the beds and everything?"

"Yes, and even in the closets."

(Laughter from him.) (I made Matthew Broderick laugh! God!)

"Okay. Well, tell her I called."

"Okay. Bye."

"Bye-bye."

I hung up. I screamed.

"I LOVE HIM!"

My mother came running out of the kitchen to make sure I was all right and that I hadn't hurt myself or been attacked by murderers. After I told her what had happened, word for word, I sat down and wrote everything to Joey. And then I called him and told him all about it.

Jennifer's house in Hidden Valley

Snow Days

Act of God: (Date 1783) an extraordinary interruption by a natural cause (as a flood or earthquake) of the usual course of events that experience, forethought, or care cannot reasonably foresee or prevent.

—*Merriam-Webster's Dictionary*

Indiana was always cold or hot, but mostly cold. We spent much of our time bundled up in sweaters and jackets and coats and scarves and gloves and mittens and boots. Of course, I never wore a hat if I could help it, because it would have ruined my hair by making it flat and small (no amount of Aqua Net could have helped it). We waddled to work and to school, through snowbanks, skidding down icy walks and streets, and God help you if you fell. You might never get up again, lying there like a fat bug, waving about until someone came along to help you up. My mom and I hated Indiana in the winter.

My parents naively bought a house with a driveway that sloped downhill. This was something neither of them thought twice about. Why would they? In Maryland the winters were civilized and polite. We weren't buried under several feet of snow. We didn't have to leave the water dripping in the faucets so that the pipes wouldn't burst. Entire trees didn't snap in half under the weight of ice.

That first Indiana winter, it snowed and snowed and snowed. And then all of that snow froze so that the entire town was encased in ice as if we were living inside a giant snow globe. It was impossible to get the cars—my dad's Jaguar and my mother's Pinto—out of the garage and up the driveway. My dad went out in the mornings and salted the *damn* driveway and shoveled the *goddamn* snow. I could hear him through the closed windows of my room swearing to himself.

Every winter it was the same thing. In the mornings, my dad was in charge of getting the *goddamn* cars up the *goddamn* hill that was our *goddamn* driveway because the realtor hadn't thought to warn us about the *goddamn* winters and tell us that we would need to move the cars onto the street in front of our house. My dad was not a morning person to begin with, so this did wonders for his already grouchy mood. And then I had to get into the car, still covered in a sheet of ice, and ride with him to school, sitting in heavy, brooding silence.

One day, after Dad had gone to work and I had gone to school—no doubt in a blizzard, because we were always being made to go to school in blizzards—my mother was home alone. At two-thirty p.m. she began the bundling process—applying layer after layer after layer, even a hat, because she never worried as much about her hair as I did about my own. At three, after what seemed like several days later, she waddled out the door to pick me up from school. A thick glaze of ice covered the car so that it looked like an enormous ice cube. She couldn't even fit the key into the lock because the lock was buried under layers of ice.

She waddled back to the house to fetch all the equipment it took to deglaze the car. My parents kept an entire elaborate kit for just this purpose, things they had acquired after years of living here. She slid the key into the front-door lock and turned it and the key snapped in half—one half in her hand, the other inside the lock. It was miserably cold. Now she couldn't get into the house and she couldn't get into the car. My poor mother was stranded outside in a day before cell phones and it was only getting colder because there was probably an ice or snowstorm on the way, as usual. She waddled from door to door, from neighbor's house to neighbor's house, and of course no one was home. She had to wander a good distance out of the neighborhood, shuffling and wobbling and overheating under all her layers yet still on the verge of frostbite, until she found a strange house on another street where someone, at last, was home to let her come in and get warm and call my father who was, naturally, in a meeting and who grumbled at being disturbed, and who never saw what the big fuss was about the cold anyway, even if he did hate snow and ice and our *goddamn* driveway. He went running year-round, in shorts and T-shirts, proudly snapping icicles off his beard when he got home.

Possibly the best thing (at times the only good thing) about growing up in Indiana was that we didn't have to make up snow days. This was because the state of Indiana believed firmly in Acts of God. The reasoning of the Indiana State Legislature was that snow and ice, like tornadoes or other natural disasters, were things one couldn't help, and therefore not something that students should be punished for.

The only problem was that this Act of God had to be a very dramatic one—perhaps one of biblical proportions—in order for us to be released from school. The morning after a large snowfall or ice storm, I would wake up early—the only time I would ever do so voluntarily—and turn on my clock radio to listen for the school closings. My room was the largest of the four bedrooms and it was bitterly cold in the mornings. I would lie there till the last possible second under the covers, soaking in the warmth.

When the school closings started, I would turn up the volume, creeping one arm out from under the blanket so fast as to not let any of the cold air in. The DJ would always start with all the other school systems: Centerville, Connersville, Fountain City, New Paris—it was maddening. Ours, because it was way down the alphabet, and the biggest, was always mentioned last, if it was mentioned at all. I would lie there in the dark, in the cold, praying to God, making little bargains with him. If he would just cancel school and let me stay home today I would clean up my room, or part of it, or at least pick up some of my clothes. I would take the dirty glasses downstairs to the kitchen, and maybe practice the piano and stick around after dinner to help with the dishes and not pretend I had to go to the bathroom like I always did.

The most wonderful sound in the world was, "And Richmond Community Schools are closed today." At which point I would turn off the radio and pull the covers up tight and close my eyes and go back to sleep for four or five hours until Joey called to talk about how wonderful it was and what was I doing and did I think we could somehow get to each other even though all the roads were closed and we lived, so it seemed to us, very far apart.

This was a problem, of course. So many of my friends lived in other neighborhoods across town, and there wasn't a way to reach them on a snow day in truly bad weather. I was isolated and really stuck at home, which was still better than being at school, and forced to hang out with people in my own neighborhood who weren't necessarily the people I hung out with at school. But if I could get to Earlham, that was fun. Because there were wonderful sledding hills. Diabolical hills that could have been used in the Olympics. Sometimes my dad took me because he drove under any condition, if he wasn't busy. Nothing scared him. And sometimes he got out on a sled himself and spun kamikaze-like down the hill and showed those kids how it was done. I met my Earlham friends there, Ruthie and Holly, and we screamed and slipped and slid and whizzed down hills with the college students and my dad, who was faster and wilder than any of them, and only then on those days would I wear a hat.

Student Life—
Part Two

"It was the best of times, it was the worst of times." And so it was inside the halls of RHS as we fought to find our place, whether it was in the cafeteria or in the classroom or on the playing field or on the dance floor. We hoped to be noticed, all the while we prayed not to stick out. At the same time we were trying to figure out who we were, we were trying to blend into the crowd. We judged and were judged on what we wore and who we knew and where we came from and where we were going. And sometimes we were judged on who we *weren't,* which was worst of all.

Joey and Jennifer

Show-and-Tell

But do they really see
What he means to me?
Do they really understand?
That although he's a man
We're just friends . . .
Just friends . . .

　　　—Jennifer McJunkin, "Just Friends," original lyrics, 1984

Teresa Ripperger had three older brothers who told her that girls who put out were sluts and girls that didn't were teases. Basically, as far as Teresa could see, it was a no-win situation if you were a girl.

Teresa thought she wouldn't have to worry about it if she stayed with one guy—Tom Dehner. This way she wouldn't be labeled a slut, and teasing was all part of the game to keep a boyfriend. Teresa and Tom met and fell in love young, back in sixth grade, back when he was shorter than she was, when her mother used to call him "Little Tommy Dehner." By the time they got to RHS, they were like a married couple.

We all hoped that when we lost our virginity it would be to the right person for the right reasons and that we wouldn't have any regrets. My best girlfriend Laura Lonigro and I talked for hours about the way it should happen and when, and the kind of boy it should be with. Laura was Italian and loud—a self-described rebel-punk-poet with spiky black hair and dark eyeliner. We were very different, but also very alike. We were both boy crazy and we loved to observe people. So naturally we looked around at our classmates and analyzed their sex lives. Most of them, as far as we could see, were having sex for the wrong reasons. Girls did it to keep boys in a relationship or to get boys. Boys did it with anyone and everyone because they thought their friends were doing it, and then they talked about the girls they did it with. We wondered where the fun was in all of this. Didn't anyone have sex just to have sex?

Teresa and Tom didn't discuss their private life with their friends. What happened between them was their business. We tried to imagine what it must be like to be Teresa, to get to be with Tom Dehner. We liked to think they were having sex all the time—after school, on the weekends, at his house, at her house, after basketball games, at dances, after dances. But we would never know because unlike some couples, they never said a word about it to anyone.

In the fall of senior year, there was a party at Fiona Ferguson's house. Fiona was from South Africa and a year behind us, and our senior year she gave a lot of parties. Joey and Jennie Burton sat in the backseat of Joey's car and the windows were steaming. Hillary Moretti and I bothered them by knocking on the glass. Finally they came out and lay down in the hammock—the one in Fiona's backyard—and Hill and I piled on top so that we all fell over onto the ground. We hung out in Fiona's garage and then later by the pool, and someone jumped in. Ned Mitchell and I made out on the dryer in the downstairs laundry room—the first and only time we were ever together—and Cliff Lester walked in on us, and then afterward a group of us gathered in the bathroom, sitting in a circle on the floor—Joey, Ned, Larry Peterson, Ian Barnes, Laura, Fiona, and me. The talk turned serious.

People thought Joey and I were a couple. This was the one question I got asked most. "So, what's up with you and Joe Kraemer?" Or, "How long have you and Joe Kraemer been together?" Or, "Have you and Joey done it yet?" I had been interrogated like this since we became friends in tenth grade.

That night on the bathroom floor, Larry said, "So tell us the truth, are you and Joey really a couple?"

Everyone looked at us, especially Ned, who wasn't sure what Joey would do if he knew we'd just been making out on a dryer.

Larry Peterson repeated his question: "So are you and Joey really a couple?"

We did what we always did in this situation. Joey put his arm around me. We smiled in a mysterious way. Joey said, "We're very close."

I said, "I love him more than anyone else."

Joey said, "She knows me better than anybody."

I said, "He's the only boy who gets me."

Joey said, "And who'll put up with her love of hairspray."

I said, "And his love of himself."

We were talking in circles around them and they knew it. Ian said, "You're not answering the question."

Joey said, "Aren't we?"

Most of us didn't have a clue about the Village People (I loved the Construction Worker) or George Michael. The first time I saw Wham's "Wake Me Up Before You Go-Go" video, I ran screaming downstairs from my bedroom to my mother to tell her I had just seen the cutest video by the cutest boys with the best hair. The only person I even had an inkling about—that something was different, that maybe he wasn't quite like other men—was Boy George, and that was only because he wore makeup and so clearly and obviously stood apart that even a blind person would have noticed it.

Joey wondered, deep in his mind, about why he didn't want to steam up car windows with Jennie or exchange candy canes with Michelle Zimmerman by mouth when they danced to "Careless Whisper" by the lights of her Christmas tree. There were many times when we let people think we were a couple because it was easier than explaining to them, or trying to explain to them, what we were to each other. We weren't sure most of them could or would really get it anyway.

Jennifer and Joey before Snowball;
Jennifer and Curt Atkisson before
Homecoming

A Dance Is Just a Dance

The dream was about Curt, and I was dating him, but then I found out your cousin Jack liked me, but there was the relationship with Curt to consider, and there was a dance and no one asked me and my outfit was see-through and my hair was sticking out badly. These are the stuffs nightmares are made of. This is the stuff from which nightmares are born.

—Jennifer to Joey, August 19, 1986

I don't understand," I told my mom when I had checked the phone connection for the fiftieth time just to make sure it was working. It was two weeks before Snowball my junior year. "Ross said Dean Waldemar liked me, that he thought I was pretty, that he was asking about me, that he wanted to know if I was free."

My mom said, "Sometimes high school boys don't ask girls out because they're afraid of rejection. He's probably afraid you'll say no."

"But I won't say no."

"But he doesn't know that. It's scary being a high school boy."

"But I won't say no!"

"But he doesn't know that and it's safer not to ask you than to ask you and be turned down."

I didn't say anything, but I was beginning to think Dean wasn't afraid of being turned down. I was beginning to think this had something to do with Tim Bullen, who I'd gone out with weeks before. When he tried to kiss me after the world's worst date, I said no, and then he told everyone at school I'd slept with him.

I asked Ross to talk to Dean again for me. Ross called me that night and said, "I hate to tell you this, but Tim Bullen told Dean some of the same lies he's been telling everybody else. Because he doesn't know you firsthand, Dean decided he's not going to ask you to Snowball and he's probably going to take someone else."

"Did you tell him Tim was lying?"

"Yes."

"What did he say?"

"He just doesn't want to mess with it."

I hung up the phone and picked up a book Joey had given me. It was a book of poetry by Suzanne Somers, which we liked to read aloud to each other. In it, he'd circled a poem called "Beautiful Girls." It was about pretty girls who were secretly lonely because they were misunderstood, usually because boys thought they were busy and never asked them out. He wrote, *Just so you know, this is why you don't always have dates every weekend.*

Instead of feeling beautiful I felt awkward and ugly. The week before Snowball, Dean asked someone else to the dance instead of me. The day before the dance, I still hadn't been asked, and Hether wrote me a cheer-up note in Humanities.

❁

Jenna Lou Anne, if no one wants you, don't worry. There are certain reasons why. Here they are:
1. It's human nature for a girl to get a break
2. Boys are not everything (no matter what you seem to think)
3. It gives you more spare time to spend with friends and family
See, there is a silver lining to every cloud.

The night of Snowball, I sat in my green room while everyone else in the world was at the dance, and wrote in my diary: *I am so tired of this place. The boy I like best of all (Matt Ashton) isn't here, and I want to be far away. Some days I don't think I can stand it much longer. I don't feel like I have anything in common with anyone other than Joey and Laura and Hether. I just want to feel—for once—like I fit in even though I want to get out of here and go somewhere else. Like Teresa or Sherri Dillon. They make it seem so easy. I wonder what it would be like to get up in the morning and be them and not have to worry about a single thing. Not that they don't have*

problems—I'm sure they do. But every day they know exactly
where they fit.

I sat at my desk and copied down poems by Walt Whit-
man, Lord Byron, Alexander Selkirk, Louisa May Alcott,
and Sara Teasdale.

These were the moments when it was hardest, when I
wished I was small and blond with a mouth full of fillings
that showed when I smiled like Jennifer Cutter who was
crowned Homecoming Queen my sophomore year, and that
I knew things like gymnastics and cheering instead of writing and music.

Our senior year, Joey asked my friend Diane Armiger to
Homecoming. He was smitten with her and her platinum
blond hair. He slipped her a note during Government class
and she wrote him back after several agonizing minutes.
Her reply said: *I have to make some phone calls. I'll tell you*
Mon. or Tues.

After she spent the weekend trying to find a more desir-
able, romantic date, she let Joey know that she would go
with him, but only as friends. She emphasized this so there
would be no mistaking it. Joey finally said, "Diane, don't
worry. I got that message when you told me you had to make
some calls before you could tell me yes."

When it was time for Snowball, Joey and I decided to
take the pressure off ourselves and go together. That way
Joey wouldn't have to worry about asking anyone and I
wouldn't have to worry about whether or not I'd be asked.

He came to pick me up for the dance—wearing navy
blue, khaki, and a red tie—in the Calais. I wore long pearls
just like Ally Sheedy in *St. Elmo's Fire*, a silky black dress
and high black heels, and a quilted satiny black coat that

had belonged to my mom's New York literary agent, who was always giving us her expensive hand-me-downs and then wanting them back at some later time.

We drove to Dayton for dinner and lost our reservations because we were late, as usual. We ran into Eric Lundquist at another restaurant, and not wanting to see him, we slunk back to Richmond, with me in my pearls and Joey in his red tie. We ended up eating at a pizza place, not at all dignified like we'd intended. Afterward, Joey bought cigarettes at a cheap gas station, and we arrived at the high school two hours late.

In the car we gulped Jack Daniel's, which Joey had stolen from his brother. It burned horribly and tasted disgusting, and we put it away after a couple of swigs. We strolled into the dance at eleven o'clock—one hour before it ended—as Angie Oler was crowned queen and Dan Dickman king. Everyone turned to look as we came in, and we were met at the door by Linda McRally, my adviser, who was hovering around sniffing for alcohol.

Out on the dance floor, Joey said, "Stumble a little now and then so Ronnie Stier will think you're drunk." Ronnie Stier was in our AP History class. He was blond, a football player, good-looking. He wore braces. We were always trying to impress him.

We loved to cause scenes, like Scott and Zelda Fitzgerald, our idols. If there had been a fountain in the RHS cafeteria like at the Plaza in New York—the one they had splashed in so famously all those years ago—we would have jumped right in. Instead I tripped into Joey and he caught me and we laughed. Ronnie turned and looked. We danced and danced. The last song was "We Built This City" by Jefferson Starship, and everyone danced together in a circle, jumping up and down and singing along. When we finally got into the spirit the lights came up and we heard the party would be at Rip's.

There was a flurry of what-to-dos and shouting and searching for coats and purses. We ended up at an all-night eatery, and then we went to the party and found ourselves in Teresa's room, the entertainment of the entire evening, Joey smoking and advising. Someone was passing around Jack Daniel's and we said no thanks, we'd had plenty. We didn't tell them that we couldn't stand the taste or mention the still-full bottle hidden in Joey's car. I did an oral inventory to all who listened of Teresa's wardrobe, while Joey dressed our hostess in his red tie, which he never saw again. Lost also were my pearls and his left penny loafer.

The downtown Promenade

Survival

It's funny—everyone here is always asking, "What was it like to grow up in a small town?" "What did you ever do for fun?" And then I usually relate some story involving water balloons or quick trips to Dayton, and after that, I kind of lose steam, and I think, Hey, what *did* we do for fun in Richmond? Did we have fun? I mean, I know we must have . . .

—*Jennifer to Joey, from Los Angeles, October 20, 1991*

Even after we were old enough to drive, there was never anything to do in Richmond. There wasn't any place to drive *to*, for one. The only places to go were the same places we had already been a thousand times, like the Skate and

the Putt-Putt and 40 Lanes. For movies, there was the Mall
Cinema, with its two screens, Cinema II with four screens,
and the Sidewalk Cinema, which was one screen in an old
theater downtown on the Promenade across from Readmore
Books, where I had once bought all my Nancy Drews, Betty
and Veronicas, and Tiger Beats.

The first movie Joey and I ever saw together was *Foot-
loose*. After that there was *Risky Business* and *Purple Rain*,
and everyone was there even though it was rated R. We
laughed through *The Legend of Billie Jean*, even though it
wasn't supposed to be funny, and we laughed so hard at *Troll*
that we were asked to leave. We fell asleep in *Pretty in Pink*,
and Jessica Howard, who was a cheerleader, had to wake
us up. Joey jumped a mile when a gun went off in *Beverly
Hills Cop* so that the people behind him snickered through
the entire film. But my favorite was *Out of Africa*, not just
because we loved the movie, but because afterward he stole
the "O" for me off the marquee as a souvenir.

Being scared was something a lot of us enjoyed, mainly
because it was so much more interesting than just about
anything else we could think up to do. On sunny weekend
afternoons or on dark nights, preferably under a full moon,
Cliff Lester picked me up in his convertible, and sometimes
Ross would be with us and Robert Ignacio, who was smaller
than the other boys and smarter than most of them. He was
the only Filipino we knew. We drove over to Crestdale to
pick up Joey and Hether Rielly. Then we drove out, out into
the country near Fair Acres to the Devil House, which was
the creepiest house outside of a Hollywood movie. It sat on
a country road, on the rise of a small hill, surrounded by
fields and corn, and which everyone knew was filled with

evil creatures, some of which were invisible. There was a long, overgrown drive under a canopy of scraggly trees that looked like people in the night, and even during the day, and we crept down this in the convertible, the windows up and the top down (Joey called it a hood).

The house itself was just a burned-out shell with only a fireplace left and skeletons of the rooms. The house was made of brick and had once been two stories. Pentagrams were spray-painted on the walls. The skulls and skins of dead animals lay scattered about the ground in a circle, up to no good. It was the scariest place in the world, even in the middle of the brightest day. Sometimes we just drove up to it and looked at it, and sometimes we got out and stood in the middle of the room with the fireplace, running away at the first strange sound.

There were other ways to scare ourselves and one another. One of Ross's brothers had constructed several enormous spotlights for a Junior Achievement project, and Ross had taken these lights for himself. The lights were so bright and big they could have guided ships home across the sea. Ross kept them in his Camaro because, as he said, "You never know when they might come in handy."

Sometimes when he was out driving, he would pull those lights out and shine them on his friends and we thought the cops were after us. He and Cliff were out one night, cruising around, when they ran across Joey and me in his mom's car, also cruising around. They pulled out the searchlights and blinded us, and those lights were so bright it was like aliens had landed, like something out of *Close Encounters*.

Joey stepped on the gas and began driving wildly through the streets, which of course made Ross start chasing us just as wildly.

"Go to Hell, Ross!" Joey shouted. We were always damning people to Hell behind their backs and sometimes to their faces. We were fascinated by Hell, Joey being a Catholic taught to fear Hell and me being a Quaker taught that Hell didn't exist.

We careened through Richmond, Cliff and Ross blinding us with those damn spotlights. They chased us through the Reid Memorial Hospital parking lot back by the old people's home, Cliff's maniacal face hanging out the passenger's side window, laughing and holding that beam steady on us.

"Park the car!" I screamed. "Pull up next to those other cars and maybe they won't notice!" Joey parked the car in a line next to a handful of other cars in the middle of a vast, dark parking lot, lit up every now and again by the glowing moon and the parking lights. We tried to duck down and hide as low as we could, as if Ross and Cliff suddenly wouldn't be able to see us, as if by parking we would become invisible. "Are they gone?" I whispered. I was truly terrified. Suddenly there was a flash of light that seemed to shine down right into the car. They were on top of us.

Joey turned the key and hit the gas without even looking. He peeled out of the parking lot and back into Crestdale and we abandoned the car in front of Laura's house, just blocks from Joey's. We fled on foot, screaming like girls, both of us, crashing this way and that through the trees and the bushes, and somehow Ross kept coming. We cut through to Joey's street, out of breath, fleeing for our lives, hearts racing, enjoying the sheer terror of it, and there came that black Camaro, roaring down on us, the spotlight growing brighter and brighter. We made it to Joey's front door, somehow, in the knick of time, scrambling to let ourselves in as Ross turned the car down Capri Lane, that spotlight coming for us. We slammed the door and looked out the window. "Assholes," Joey said. Ross pulled into the driveway and honked the horn. We went outside and got in the car and went for pizza.

On the night of the water balloons, there was a party at Eric Ruger's house, way out in the country. His parents were always there, keeping out of the way. Every now and then his dad would appear at the window or just outside, hands on hips, to make sure we were okay. His mother stayed inside. She was pretty and had a nice smile, but someone said she'd had an aneurysm once. I had never met anyone with an aneurysm, and it made me want to look at her closely or stay far away in case it might happen again.

Jennie Burton drove her station wagon. Joey and Hill and Hether and I were there, and it was Joey's idea to buy some balloons and fill them with water. We went to the party for a while, but by that time it was all the same people and we were tired of them and ready for a change. Joey and I bought the balloons at a thrift store and said they were for our children. We stopped at Jennie's house to fill them with water, and then we loaded them in the back of her car, where Hill and Joey sat by the window.

We drove out in the country and ended up by Eric Ruger's. The party was still going on, but just as we passed by, Cliff Lester pulled out of the drive in his convertible, the same one that had carted us to the Devil House. Jennie lowered the back window and Joey threw the first balloon, which flew into Cliff's windshield and smashed, water going everywhere. Crazy Vicki Mulla was with him and she immediately started yelling.

Joey fired one balloon after another and Cliff chased us around town for two hours, running through every light and over curbs to catch us. He drove with his head out the window screaming, "Jennie Burton! I know it's you! Stop it! Stopitstopitstopitstopit!!!" in that crazed baby-shriek of his. Jennie swerved through downtown, out toward the country again, then back into town, this time over on the east side by the mall. Sometimes when we went over bumps, the balloons exploded, soaking us all. Cliff drove like a demon, pulling up as close as he could to Jennie's bumper. Hether and I screamed and Hill swore and Joey kept hurling balloons until we ran out.

Before they gave up, Vicki Mulla leaned her whole body out the window and cursed us out. After we finally, somehow, lost Cliff, we pulled into Burger King to fill the remaining balloons with water. Jennie waited in the car while Hill and Hether and Joey and I went inside. Tom Dehner and Teresa were there with Leigh Torbeck and Todd Irwin. We were soaking wet and laughing and my mascara was running. Rip waved us over.

"What the hell have you guys been doing?" she said. She was staring at our wet clothes, at the balloons.

"Oh, just driving," Joey said.

"Can I use your napkin?" I said to Todd. He handed me Leigh's napkin by mistake and her retainer fell out onto the floor. She turned bright red. "There is nothing so important as a healthy mouthful of teeth," I said, and I picked the retainer up with the napkin and handed it back to her. Then Hill, Hether, and I went to the bathroom to fill up more balloons while Joey stayed and talked.

"Why is your group always sneaking about?" Tom Dehner wanted to know.

"Because the most interesting evenings can only be found if one sneaks about," Joey said.

Back in the car, Jennie drove over to Reeveston, where she and Ross and Cliff and Rip and Dehner and almost every other popular person lived. We cruised by Cliff Lester's giant colonial house with the outdoor lighting and the four garages and then sat idling in the shadows. His car wasn't there and he always parked in the driveway, so we knew he wasn't home yet. Joey grabbed the largest of the balloons and ran across the street to the side entrance of Cliff's house. There, beneath the yellow bulb that shone on the doorstep, he placed the water balloon where he knew Cliff would find it. Hill held the car door open for Joey to jump back in, and Jennie floored it, brakes squealing as she peeled away from the crime scene. We drove around for another hour before she took us home.

On Monday morning, Jennie told us that someone had trashed her car. We knew it was Cliff, but Jennie couldn't tell her dad because then we'd have to tell him about the water balloons. Jennie's dad was older than regular parents and a lawyer, and we didn't think he would understand.

Someone getting pulled over on National Road

Law and Order

We had so many horrible times in traffic didn't we, because we could never figure out how it was supposed to work?

—*Joey to Jennifer, May 3, 1996*

One night when there were no parties and no football games and no one we knew was doing anything interesting and I was in between boyfriends, Joey picked me up in his mom's car and we drove to Earlham College. I had just begun to make friends with some of the freshman soccer and lacrosse players there, boys named Shane and Tim and Bill.

The campus was quiet and dark and nobody was out. We drove to the very back of it, back behind the student center, back by the soccer fields, which were empty. There was a turnaround there—a large circle surrounding a grassy center.

We cranked up the stereo—Prince's "Let's Go Crazy"—and began driving round and round the circle as fast as we could. We sang and screamed at the top of our lungs like we were on a ride at King's Island Amusement Park, the Calais making those turns over and over like a race car at the Indianapolis 500.

This went on for at least two rounds of "Let's Go Crazy"—possibly more—before Joey hit the curb and the tire blew out. Because neither of us knew the first thing about cars or tires or what to do when something like this happened (my dad had once explained it to me, but because I didn't drive myself I hadn't paid attention), we sat there in the dark and then stood there in the dark, trying to figure out what in the world to do.

"Goddammit," Joey said.

"Yes," I said.

We were faced with the same thing we were always faced with: we had done something to the car and now we were going to have to call someone. But which parent? My parents were closer in proximity, but we were at Earlham. *Where my dad worked*. Where we had just been driving like we were in the Indy 500, blasting Prince and screaming like maniacs.

It was after midnight and past my curfew. Joey's parents were across town. Mr. Kraemer would be furious. He had already been grumbling about taking the car away from Joey after our last run-in with a flat tire and a brick on the interstate. Mrs. Kraemer would just call my mother and tell her what happened.

We stood there for at least twenty minutes and tried to make up our minds.

When it was clear the tire wasn't going to fix itself and no one was going to magically appear to help us, we walked into Runyon Center, which was dark and quiet, and found a pay phone and called Mr. Kraemer. I could hear him through the receiver as Joey held the phone from his ear and rolled his eyes at me. Joey hung up and said, "He's on his way." We sat down on the curb in the dark, the stars twinkling overhead—every one of them visible, as they are in the wide Indiana sky—and waited.

"I have got to learn to change a tire," Joey said.

"Maybe we should take Auto Shop," I said. "With the smokers and the hoods." Some of them were good-looking. Okay, one or two of them. I was good at Metal Shop in junior high. I wondered how different Auto Shop could be.

We chattered on about that possibility, so easily distracted, until Mr. Kraemer showed up. We saw the headlights of his car coming from a half mile away. He got out of the car and smiled and shook his head—on his warmest behavior for me. I thought of my own father, and how he wouldn't have smiled or acted nice at all about this. He wouldn't have said a word, just gone right to work on that tire like I wasn't even there. Mr. Kraemer made jokes and called Joey "Buddy" and scolded us a little and asked us what in the world we'd been doing to hit that curb.

After they dropped me off, when they got back home, Mr. Kraemer threatened to take the car away from Joey. This, of course, was not the first time something like this had happened while Joey was driving. And it wouldn't be the last. Mr. Kraemer clearly knew that. But Joey was persuasive. He promised to be more responsible, to be better, more careful. We wouldn't drive in circles anymore. We would watch the road for bricks. Joey would be a model driver, someone his dad could count on.

Joey had a way about him. Parents and teachers wanted

to trust him. Even when he did things like rip the pages from Mr. Brumley's math book and change our grades in Mr. Foos's grade book, they looked at his sweet, cherubic face, the glasses, the halo of blond hair, and believed that he had only the best intentions.

He got to keep the car.

One week later, we were driving back from Dayton in the Calais. We had been to one of our favorite destinations—the Dayton Mall—where we shopped and ate hot pretzels with cheese and just got the hell out of Richmond for a while. On the way home, we drank chocolate chip milk shakes from Rax and listened to Billy Idol and Madonna and a few of our other favorites—the Police, Adam Ant, the Clash, Talking Heads, and Peter Gabriel's "Big Time" (which we felt was written for us)—and then we decided to see what was on the radio. This was something we didn't often do, but while Joey drove, keeping his eyes responsibly on the road, I searched through the handful of radio stations, even the AM ones.

As we crossed under the blue Ohio arch into Indiana and took the exit that would lead us right into Richmond, we heard it: the beginning strains of an instrumental song, tinny and scratchy, on one of the AM stations. The sole instrument was piano, and it plunked along somberly, an unrecognizable tune.

As we passed Bob Evans and the Putt-Putt Golf, Joey began to sing: "Back again in Richmond, where the people all drive slow . . ."

Without missing a beat, I joined him, making up the next line: "Back again in Richmond, where the people never go."

We went on, inventing words to the entire song. I happened to have a tape recorder in the car because sometimes I liked to record our conversations for our future biographers. With luck, it was on when we began to sing.

"It's got a tiny skyscape, and the people are happy here . . ."

We flew by Fred First Ford, the movie theater, Mr. G's Hairstyling and Lounge, the Richmond Square Mall, Burger King, Long John Silver's, and the Target parking lot where the usual Trans Ams and Corvettes were lined up, kids sitting on bumpers, drinking and laughing. We spun past the Arboretum and Glen Miller Park, and past the Promenade. We turned down North A Street and drove past Morrisson-Reeves Library, Le Crazy Horse Salon, and the *Palladium-Item*.

Billy Idol was back on the stereo. Joey was driving wildly, but neither of us cared or noticed. We were carried away as usual—by the music, by each other. We were young and invincible. We were bored out of our minds and the town couldn't contain us. We were wild and free. Joey took a drink from his milk shake, draining it, and hurled it out the window.

We were just careening around the corner by Swayne-Robinson, an abandoned, burned-out old factory (former maker of farm machinery) on the corner of North A Street and Main, when, above the sound of our singing and the sound of tires squealing, we heard the siren. In the rearview mirror and in the side mirrors—everywhere suddenly—we could see flashing lights.

"Is that for me?" Joey yelled.

I was checking all the mirrors. I turned around over the seat and stared out the back window. "Yes!"

"Goddammit!"

"Oh my God!"

"What do I do?!"

We were hysterical. In all of our many driving adventures, we had, unbelievably, never been pulled over before. Billy Idol was still screaming and we didn't think to turn him down. We screamed over him.

"Pull over!" I said.

"Where?!" Joey looked around frantically and swerved across two lanes.

"Turn down the next street!" I pointed. "There!"

We crossed the Main Street Bridge, passing Pizza King where I recognized people from school just outside and in the parking lot. Joey didn't even bother stopping at the red light. He shot straight on through, turned right (without using a signal), and finally came to a stop. The police car pulled up behind us, lights flashing.

We turned off the stereo. The night grew silent. We sat there waiting, both of us too petrified to talk or move. In a moment the policeman appeared in the window. He was a big man. In the dark, he seemed like a giant. He peered in, looking first at Joey, then at me. He said, "Son, I'm going to need you to step out of the car and come with me." It was like a scene out of a scary movie or an Afterschool Special.

Joey fumbled with the door and finally, with the policeman's help, got it open and followed him to the police car. I sat there imagining all of the horrible things that must be happening right that minute to my very best friend. What if he was being arrested? What if the cop was booking him right now and reading him his rights? What if he was going to take Joey to jail? What if I had to call Joey's parents from the Wayne County Safety Building, where the jail was located, and tell them what happened? What if I had to drive Joey's car there myself? This was almost the worst thought of all because I hadn't driven once since getting my license, since the nightmare of Driver's Ed. And then I thought of something far worse: *What if we were both going to be expelled and now I would never graduate Richmond High School but have to live in this town forever?*

As I sat there—as Joey sat behind me in the squad car—cars were slowing down and passing us. One car kept circling, going around the block and coming back again. Rhonda Treadway was behind the wheel and Bea McGraw, Joey's tenth-grade Homecoming date, was sitting beside her. They were smirking and laughing. They kept circling around and coming back, inching past us.

After about fifteen minutes, Joey reappeared. He opened the door and sat down beside me and buckled his seat belt and flipped on his turn signal and checked all his mirrors, and then he pulled out into the street—as the policeman watched—and headed toward my house.

He said, "I hope I see Bea McGraw have problems with a police car one day, but instead of being *in* one, I hope she's *under* one."

We looked. They were gone.

"What happened?" I said. It came out very low, like a whisper.

"The cop said, 'Look, I don't want to embarrass you in front of your girlfriend, but when you're driving a car, you've got to be responsible. A vehicle is not a toy. You can't just be trying to impress the pretty little lady.' And then he gave me a lecture on driving maturely and safely."

"That's it?"

"No." Joey pulled out a piece of paper and handed it to me. *A ticket.* "He listed every violation he saw me make.

They included littering—when I threw my cup out of the car. Running two red lights. Turning left on red—is that illegal?"

"I keep telling you that."

"Going fifty-five in a thirty-mile-per-hour zone. Running a stop sign. Reckless driving. Going the wrong way down a one-way street."

"What one-way street?"

"I have no idea. Driving without my license. Neglecting to stop when he first turned on his light—but I wasn't going to stop in the middle of all those people where we could be laughed at! And not staying in my lane. He said to me, 'Son, if I totaled up everything I saw you do wrong in the past five minutes, it would cost you over $300 and you'd be close to losing your license, so I'm going to let you choose two of these violations.'"

"Oh my God." I was in awe. This was my very first run-in with the law unless you counted the time Joey and I had gotten lost in Indianapolis and had to go to a police station there for help (and Joey had stolen the cap from the officer who helped us, but was so scared afterward that we left it in RHS Assistant Principal Sandra Hillman's unlocked car in front of her house). Until that moment, what we knew about cops was who was on duty and where they lived.

I had a newfound respect for our men in blue. "That was so nice of him," I said. "What did you choose?"

"Exceeding the speed limit and running a stop sign. Who would have believed I was really driving seriously?"

We drove home quietly, sedately. We left the stereo off. We sang softly to ourselves, repeating what we remembered of "Back Again in Richmond." Joey obeyed almost every traffic law.

Jeff Shirazi's Volkswagen Bug

Politics

Finally our senior year is over with.
I don't think I could stand much more.
The yearbook only tells me one thing:
people don't matter unless they are popular.

—*Becky Scheele, November 14, 1986*

When we were moving to Richmond, my parents narrowed down their house search to two houses—one in Hidden Valley and one in Reeveston. The one in Reeveston looked like a small gothic castle, complete with a turret. The house had a large pink bedroom that was perfect for me, and, best of all, a tiny maid's room above the kitchen at the top of a hidden staircase. In my opinion, this was better than a secret tunnel or a cave because it was almost sure to hold a mystery. I really, really wanted that house.

In the end, though, my parents decided on the Hidden Valley house because it was closer to Earlham College and my dad's work, and it had a much larger backyard for me to play in, with a creek and woods. I liked the Hidden Valley house, loved my enormous green room, which was twice as big as the pink one, but as I grew older I understood the significance of my parents' decision. It was a significance none of us could have appreciated at the time: if they had bought the Reeveston house instead—which they almost did, which they came *this* close to doing—I would have gone to Test Junior High School. The *this close* factor of it all took my breath away.

What would my life have been like if I had gone to Test instead of Dennis? Would I have been a member of the Homecoming court every year like Sherri Dillon and Leigh Torbeck? Would Tom Dehner have noticed me first, before he ever met Teresa Ripperger? Would Tom and I have arrived at the high school as *the* power couple, a force to be reckoned with? Would I have had a cool nickname like Rip and thrown parties every weekend? Would I have ever needed to worry about fitting in, about being popular? Would everything in my life have been effortless and easy? Would I have had better hair?

On the days when high school was at its worst, when it really and truly couldn't be stood, I sat in my green room in Hidden Valley on the wrong side of town and blamed my parents for buying the wrong house.

The town of Richmond was conservative. The local college was liberal. Being an Earlham kid raised in a liberal, freethinking household, I didn't think twice about shooting my mouth off over my political views. Not that I followed politics or had a deep interest in it, but I did overhear my parents talking about the state of things, and I had once— sadly, misguidedly—voted for Nixon in my preschool class simply because his name sounded similar to my middle name, Niven.

It was important to be Republican and Catholic in Richmond. With the presidential election approaching, people in my high school class—those who lived in Reeveston and came from money—trashed Walter Mondale and talked about Ronald Reagan as though they knew him, repeating things about him that you just knew they had heard their parents say.

My parents weren't crazy about Walter Mondale, but they certainly didn't like Ronald Reagan. All I knew was that Reagan would be a bad, bad president. Whenever Tom Mangas and Curt Atkisson and any of my other friends got started about Reagan and how poor Mondale would suffer the defeat he deserved come November, I talked back. I went on and on about Walter Mondale as if he were Tom Petersson of Cheap Trick.

On election night, I was in my room reading and watching television and listening to music, all of which I liked to do simultaneously. (This made my father crazy.) It was late, and the returns were still coming in, but it seemed pretty clear that Reagan was going to win. My mom was downstairs and my dad was still at Earlham. The air had turned bitter almost overnight, unseasonably cold even for November.

Over all the noise in my room, there was the distant thud of a car door slamming. I kept reading and eventually got up to turn off the TV and turn down the stereo. From outside, I heard voices. I opened the blinds of one of the two front windows. At first, I thought it had snowed. The trees were white and the lawn was white. But then I looked closer and it wasn't snow, but toilet paper. There were dark figures crouched in our yard and swinging from our trees. My heart did a little leap.

I knew that Teresa Ripperger and Tom Dehner and the whole gang of them were always TP-ing one another's houses. Jeff Shirazi had told me about a time when an entire group of them drove out to his house at two in the morning and Rip and everyone started throwing toilet paper everywhere until Jeff ran out screaming. He said it scared them to death, and he just laughed and laughed as they drove away.

We had never had our house TP-ed. I consoled myself by thinking about how far out our house was, on the other side of town from Rip and Dehner and all the rest of them. Sometimes at Halloween, the boys from my neighborhood TP-ed a tree or two, but these were boys like Duane Rooks and Gary Greenwalter who took Auto Shop and hung out in the Smokers Hall.

It was beginning to look like a blizzard outside when there was, suddenly, a flash of silver from the street. I watched in horror as my father pulled up in front of the house and climbed out of the car, dressed in one of his impeccable and expensive custom-tailored business suits. He was carrying his briefcase, and at the curb he stopped and yelled something. All the dark figures scattered in five directions, and just like Superman, my father, in his suit and spectacles, threw down his briefcase and began running after them.

I watched, helpless, from the window, unable to stop

him. I heard a male voice scream, "Mr. McJunkin is coming!" And then the unmistakable putt-putt-putt of a VW Bug speeding away.

I was sick. What had my father done? I sat there for a long time on my green floor, and then I thought about calling Joey, but realized it was after midnight and I didn't want to wake his parents. I went downstairs.

My mother was looking out the living room window, puzzled. "Have you seen this?" she said, waving at the yard.

"Where's Dad?" I asked.

"I don't know."

"Dear God," I said. Because I somehow knew, but didn't know, who might be behind this. I only knew one person who drove a VW Bug, and it was too wonderful and impossible to even think that he might come all the way out to my house and go to the trouble of TP-ing it.

Mom and I stood there, staring out the window. We stood there for several long minutes—more like hours— until the front door opened, and my father walked in. His face was shiny, damp, and flushed, and he was grinning like a wicked, angry devil.

"I chased them out to National Road," he said.

My eyes grew wide. "National Road?" That was at least a mile away.

"One of them fell into the Blakeys' pool."

"Was he hurt?" my mother asked.

"There was still water in it," he said.

"How many of them were there?" I said, my voice barely a whisper.

"Five, maybe six." My dad pulled back the curtain and stared outside as if he had special night vision that allowed him to see in the dark. "I scared the hell out of them." He looked at my mom, triumphant. "And I got the license plate of the get-away car. It said 'JPS.'"

"What?" I said. My heart stopped beating for one full minute and then began doing flips.

"'JPS,'" my dad repeated.

"Like *Jeff Shirazi?!*" My voice came out loud and high. From the kitchen, our dog Tosh started barking.

"I suppose," my dad said.

"*Jeff Shirazi TP-ed my house?!*" I threw the door open and ran outside in my bare feet. The trees dripped with white. The lawn was completely covered so that the green of the grass showed through only in patches. Little trails of white paper waved like flags from the bushes and the gutters. It must have taken rolls and rolls of toilet paper. There was shaving cream on the ground. *"Jeff Shirazi did this?!"* I was shouting by this time, so loud that the neighbors were sure to hear.

"What is wrong with her?" my dad asked my mom. They were standing on the front step.

I started dancing and leaping about. And then slowly, just like a windup toy unwinding, I came to a stop. "What do you mean you chased them?"

"I chased them out to National Road, up to Frisch's," my dad said. He meant Frisch's Big Boy with the sign out front that always read *Try our Cheery Pie* because the man who changed the letters was slow. "Except for the one who fell into the pool and the one who drove away."

My heart stopped again and my breath stopped. I stood blinking at him. "How could you do this to me?" I said finally, when I had recovered my ability to speak. I rarely confronted my father or talked back to him, but I couldn't help myself. He had chased, on foot, *Jeff Shirazi* and God knows who else. He had run them down like some mad, wild dog in a suit.

I stomped into the house and ran up to my room and slammed my door. As I ran, I heard my dad say to my mom, "What in the hell is wrong with her?"

The very best thing to ever happen to me, and my dad had ruined it. This was what happened, I told myself, when you had a father who ran marathons. My dad ran eight or nine miles a day—a *day*—and twenty-six on the weekends. He was a maniac. Until now, it had never interfered with my life. He went for his runs, sometimes with Tosh, sometimes alone, and he came back sweaty and hungry, and, depending on the season, would either complain about it being "hot as the Devil," or would have to cut the icicles from his beard. My mother and I endured the complaints and the sore muscles, the knee that sometimes gave him problems, and the midnight snacks that my father made in secret, or so he thought. They stank up the entire house for days—fat Bavarian sausages fried up at the stove while he smoked his pipe and drank a glass of wine, thinking no one could smell the onions. But this . . . this was too much to bear.

I raised the blind and looked out the front window. In the center of the lawn, right beneath my room, I could tell that the shaving cream spelled something. I rubbed the glass where my breath had made a cloud, and looked. *Regan*, it said in crooked white letters.

Idiots, I thought. *They could have at least spelled it right.*

Indiana cornfields

Signs

This goes out to the person or persons that found it necessary to take a wreath from a grave. Every time you look at this wreath remember one day someone you love will be buried and when someone carries your flowers away as you have done, you won't be able to say a word, will you!

—*Mary Ann Harrison,* Palladium-Item, *"Your Opinion" section*

Sandra Hillman was assistant principal of Richmond High School. Joey and I once filled her van with helium balloons, as many as we could fit, and laughed till we cried picturing her face as she opened the door and all those balloons sailed away. We thought it would be a lovely scene, like something from a movie—*Out of Africa* or *Trip to Bountiful,* both of which we'd loved. It would be almost like poetry.

It was just something we thought up to do, like climbing the Purina Tower or driving fast in circles or writing stories about how we were separated at birth, creating an entire elaborate backstory for ourselves in which we were stolen from our original (shared) parents and smuggled across the world through a series of wild and dangerous adventures only to end up in the World's Most Boring Town. In other words, we didn't do it to be mean.

But there were some things that our classmates did do to teachers to get back at them for unfair exams, for pop quizzes, for picking on them in class, or for just trying to do their jobs. One of these things was to steal realty signs and, in the dark of night, stick them in their front yards. Some teachers woke up on weekend mornings to find seven or eight For Sale signs—possibly more—on their lawns, depending on how unreasonable they had been in class that week.

Collecting signs was a popular activity. My friend Hillary always carried a tool kit in her purse along with her lipstick and her tampons, just in case she saw a sign she liked. She had a particular love for license plates—not stealing them, but switching them from car to car. She could spend a happy hour in a parking lot, usually one at a church.

On one rare night when there weren't any parties, Joey and I found ourselves, as usual, driving up and down the streets of Reeveston. We even drove way out in the country to where Ian Barnes lived in a multilevel wooden house by a pond. There was a diving board that hung over the water that someone always jumped off of around midnight when there was a party. But on this particular night the pond was dark and the house was quiet.

"Should we go out to Ruger's?" I said hopefully.

"No," Joey said. "He's out of town this weekend."

"What about Jeff's?"

"He's probably holed up somewhere with Angie." Jeff Shirazi and Angie Oler had been dating off and on for almost a year.

We drove aimlessly. I didn't have to be home for two hours.

"We could call Jennie and Hill and see if they want to meet us somewhere," I said.

"No. Hillary's a pill and I don't want to see Jennie right now." Joey and Jennie had been going out for a few weeks. She was always trying to climb on him and get him to do things to her that he didn't want to do. "We could steal signs," Joey said.

I thought about this. I never wanted to get caught stealing signs, but there was nothing else to do. "I guess."

We cruised around for half an hour or so on dark, dusty roads, in the thick of farm country. These were where the best signs could be found—funny, colorful signs stuck in cornfields or vegetable patches, or tacked to the outside of barns.

We drove slowly down Backmeyer Road, going fast over the hills so that the car bounced, and then slowing down in the flat parts. We listened to Billy Idol's "White Wedding," which seemed appropriate for committing acts of delinquency.

We headed out to Mr. Kaiser's farm, south of Boston, which was far, far away from anything. To me, who didn't drive, who thought all farms and cornfields looked the same, it seemed hundreds of miles from Richmond, though it was probably more like seven. Joey had spent each summer working for the Kaisers, bailing hay and painting the barn and doing other farm-type chores. We drove out onto the property, which seemed enormous and had a grand name like Marlando.

At the front of the grounds there was a little trailer with a light on inside, which Joey said was just a decoy to discourage trespassers. Mr. Kaiser and his wife wanted people to think they had a groundskeeper. There was something very lonely about it. We drove past the decoy trailer all the way to the back of the property, which was thick with high, dark trees and a swing. We got out of the car and stood there, listening to the stillness. Far off in the distance you could see the burning orange glow of Richmond.

I sat down in the swing and Joey started pushing me. We stared out at the view of the town.

"From here it looks almost pretty," Joey said.

"One day we'll be far, far away from it," I said. "I wonder where."

"New York. Moscow. Dublin."

"Paris. London. Los Angeles."

We named all the cities of the world that weren't in the Midwest, Joey pushing me higher and higher, and then we climbed back into the car and drove even farther out into the country. The moon was out and the stars were white-bright and we turned the headlights off because we didn't need any lights other than what was in the sky.

Then, coming around a corner, we saw *the* sign. It was enormous and white and glowed in the moonlight. It stood near the side of the road by the edge of a cornfield, and the farmhouse sat several yards away, blank and quiet. I thought of the farmer and his family who were no doubt asleep inside, early to bed, early to rise. I felt a little pang.

We drifted toward the sign. *AgriGold*, it said in black letters. And above it, a lively cartoon drawing of an ear of corn, bright yellow with green husks. I caught my breath. Close up, the sign was even bigger than it first looked. It was taller than I was and taller than Joey. It was as tall as Ross. It was maybe even taller than that.

I had been terrified of corn ever since we watched *Children of the Corn* at Joey's house, required viewing for any Indiana teenager. We loved to scare ourselves by driving out into the country in the dead of night and then turning off the headlights and driving directly into the corn. Joey and I did this night after night, but it always ended the same way—with one of us seeing a face in the rearview mirror or there to the left, to the right, over there in the corn.

Joey pulled past the farmhouse, past the AgriGold sign (AgriGold, it said on one side; AgriGold it said on the other), and parked near the edge of the cornfield. We rolled down the windows and sat listening to the night.

"Okay," Joey said. "Let's go."

I was nervous. "Why don't I just wait here?" I said. "I'll keep watch."

"Are you scared of getting caught?"

"Yes."

He rolled his eyes at me. Then he bundled up the tools in his shirt and climbed out of the car. As the door opened, the inside of the car immediately lit up.

"Don't slam the door!" I hissed. "Just close it enough so that the light goes off."

I watched him in the rearview mirror as he walked around back. I slunk down low in my seat and watched him in the side mirror. He bent over, setting the tools on the ground, no doubt trying to figure out what was what. My eyes moved back and forth between the farmhouse and Joey, the farmhouse and Joey.

I stuck my head out the window. "What are you doing?" I whispered, as loud as I could.

"Trying to figure out how to get the sign down."

I got out of the car, careful not to slam the door. "Let me see." I examined the bolts that anchored the sign to its posts. I examined our tools. "This one, I think." I handed him a wrench. "And this one." I handed him a screwdriver. We bumped each other and dropped some things and there were crickets hopping in the grass, which caused us both to jump and scream. The corn rustled and we stood very still, waiting.

I tiptoed back to the car. I slunk back down against the seat and watched him. *Hurry*, I thought. *Hurryhurryhurry-hurry.*

Twenty minutes later, Joey had undone the bolts at the bottom of the sign, and was climbing up the side to reach the top. I sat there shivering, even though it was still hot and sticky out, offering up little prayers that we would get home safely. I thought of Demi Moore in *St. Elmo's Fire* and how fearless she was. I thought of Zelda Fitzgerald diving into fountains and dancing on tables. I was trying very hard to be fearless, too.

At some point, there was a crash, as Joey and not one but two AgriGold signs hit the earth. They had been hitched together, back to back, one showing one way, one showing the other. I popped the trunk and jumped out of the car.

"Get your sign!" he shouted.

We each grabbed hold of one and dragged them toward

the car, running smack into each other, our heads knocking, the signs making a metal *boi-oi-oing* sound.

"Put them in!" I shrieked.

It took both of us to lift each one, but somehow we got them into the trunk. The trunk wouldn't close, but we threw Joey's sweatshirt on top of the signs, so that they would be at least partially disguised. Joey drove me home with the trunk door bobbing up and down. He drove under the speed limit and was extra cautious.

The next morning, Joey's dad went into the garage and found the AgriGold signs propped against a wall.

Joey was still asleep, but his dad rapped on his door and then walked right in. "Hey, Buddy?" he said. "Where did those giant corn signs come from?"

From his bed, Joey didn't say anything, just pulled the covers up over his head and tried to go on sleeping.

"You and Jennifer didn't steal them did you?"

From under his pillow, Joey said, "Mitchell." Mitchell was Joey's brother who was a year younger than we were. "Mitchell and his delinquent friends probably took them."

Of course Mr. Kraemer knew this was a lie. Mitchell, for the most part, was much better behaved than we were. "You know they have cameras out there, keeping an eye on those signs. Those farmers are always getting things stolen from them and that's their way of making sure they're protected. Whoever took those signs will be on videotape. They could be turning those tapes over to the police even as you're lying there in your bed. I guess I should go downstairs now and wait for the phone to ring. What do you want me to tell them?"

Joey lifted the pillow off his face. "What do you mean they have cameras? You're just making that up."

Mr. Kraemer said, "Am I?" He let Joey think about this. "I'm surprised you didn't see the cameras actually. But then again, the farmers hide them in the corn." He walked out the door then and left the room. By this time Joey was wide awake. He reached for the phone and dialed my number.

Alex Delaney

First Heartbreak

If we cannot find the road to
happiness, let's make one!

—*Alex Delaney*

A lex Delaney came into my life the fall of my junior year.
He was a popular senior with a tangled mane of curly
gold hair and bright blue eyes. He was California cute, right
in the middle of landlocked Richmond, Indiana. We had
Humanities class together and began to cast longing, elec-
trically charged glances across the room at each other until
I couldn't stand it anymore. If he had been Tommy Wissel
or Tom Mangas, I would have just written him a coy little
note (Me: *Tommy, I think marriage would be wonderful, but
being your mistress sounds like fun. I wouldn't want Suzanne to
find out and I wouldn't want to disrupt a marriage—but don't*

I have a nice chest? Tommy: *Yes, what I can see of it. I can't tell real well though. But maybe if I had a chance to see it better I would know.* Me: *You're pretty sly, aren't you? Now let me think. When would you get a chance? I could move over a seat so you could have a better view, but that probably wouldn't be much better. Any suggestions?*)

But Alex was different. Alex seemed worlds older than anyone I had dated before. He moved in an orbit far beyond the one I knew. He was best friends with John Dehner, Tom Dehner's older brother. Alex was a senior. He was *experienced.* The whole idea of him was vaguely unnerving. Visions of Freddie Prinze, my first true love, with his tight jeans and wicked smile, came to mind.

I wrote my friend Holly Ogren a note in AP History class. Jennifer: *Tell me about Alex!*

Holly: *I don't know him very well, but from what I know of him he's really sweet. Diane Weigle went with him for a long time. That's about the extent of my knowledge.*

I knew all about Alex's previous relationship with Diane, a pretty redheaded senior. She was smart and nice and well-liked. She wasn't an ex-girlfriend you could hate like Carrie Hockersmith. She and Alex had been together for a Very Long Time, but had recently broken up. I was just single myself. Curt Atkisson and I had split up not long after Homecoming.

Finally, after two weeks of meaningful glances in Humanities, one of Alex's friends got sick of our silent pining and decided to get us together. Alex asked me out, staring at the ground the entire time, and I said yes, staring at my feet.

On our first date, Alex picked me up in his little red Toyota and took me out on the town for dinner and a movie. He was shy and I was shy and I thought how weird this was since I liked flirting with boys almost as much as I liked writing stories or singing into my hairbrush and pretending I was a rock star or driving fast with Joey to the Dayton Mall. I thought, *Heaven help us. We will never get through this night.*

In the movie his arm inched closer to mine, brushing against it on the armrest. I had been through this dance many times before and knew what to do. If I didn't want him to hold my hand, all I had to do was put my hands in my lap. If I wanted him to hold it, all I needed to do was leave it there on the armrest and let him take over. I left it there. He moved his closer. This went on for most of the movie until finally our fingers touched and then he took my hand.

After that, our shyness went away. On the way home, we laughed a lot. He was funny. We talked over each other. By the end of the evening, we were kissing in his car. Kissing was what we were best at.

There was another date. And another after that. He always called me when he said he would. We talked for hours on the phone every night until my mother told me to hang up, that it was time for bed. It wasn't long before we were going together. He walked me to classes and wrote me notes. I wrote him notes back. I wrote him a poem. He wrote me one. He called me "Gorgeous." He told me he loved me. I told him I loved him.

Jen, I have 10 minutes left in Analysis and this empty sheet of paper, so I thought I'd brighten your day. I realized that last night made a big difference (or maybe just this whole last week) in the way I feel and/or think about us. It's a good feeling, a feeling of closeness and intimacy, and I love it. I hope that you maybe feel the same way! Put a smile on your face and remember: I love you, Al

I wondered if this was what grown-up love felt like. I had loved Eric Lundquist, but that seemed young and innocent compared to this. Love with Eric was sweet and heady and giddy. It left me light-headed and breathless. Love with Alex made me want to put my head between my knees and throw up into the trash can. It felt painful and exhilarating at once, like being on an upside-down roller coaster or slamming your finger in the car door. I always felt slightly unhinged, like I wasn't in control, something I hated.

I met his brothers (all blond, too many to keep track of) and he talked to me about his parents, who didn't get along and were always fighting. I felt bad for him because my own parents were happy. They never argued and always got along and the three of us liked to do things as a family, like go out to eat or to the movies, or on trips to Cincinnati or Chicago, when my dad wasn't too busy working at the college.

Alex and I did our homework together and tried hard to study without falling into and onto and on top of each other. Inevitably, we always wound up engaging in fierce make-out sessions in his basement or in my basement, which left both of us angry and excited and wound up for days.

We talked about sex all the time. He knew I wanted to wait to do it till some unforeseen time in the future. I wasn't sure when this would be exactly, but I was sure the time would make itself known to me, that there would be a magic moment when all the stars aligned and I would just . . . *know.*

Hey, Gorgeous—I know that I tell you that you look good all the time, but today you look great! That outfit looks so good on you! It's unique and I like it a whole lot! I only wish I could touch you and hold you with you feeling comfortable, but for you, I will force myself not to (Maybe!). Love ya, Al

My dad, as if he sensed what was going on, never said much to Alex. At least he let him inside the house, which was an improvement. When Alex said, "I don't think your dad likes me," I cheerfully pointed out that he hadn't been made to wait outside on the front step. A week or so into our relationship we were even allowed downstairs in the family room with the door closed, which was amazing. One night we heard the door open and my dad started down the stairs. Alex and I broke apart and sat chastely beside each other on the couch, our hearts pounding. My dad stomped down the stairs without stomping—a gift he had perfected. He didn't say a word. He walked by us to his stereo, fussed about with his albums, and then, again without saying a word or retrieving a single item, walked by us and went back upstairs.

"Your dad is good," Alex said. "It's like he came down here and peed on you and he didn't even have to say anything."

We watched TV the rest of the night without touching.

We went to basketball games together. It was the most exciting time in history for RHS basketball, because after years of being mediocre, of never ever winning a state championship in a state that worships basketball, the Red Devils won sectionals. Then we won regionals. Then we advanced to our first state finals in thirty-two years. Even I was excited.

Although we did things with Alex's friends (which was thrilling, especially when John Dehner was around because, like his younger brother, he was so effortlessly cool), most of the time Alex agreed to do things with my friends because that was what I wanted. He would invite Joey over to sit with us in his basement and listen to music or watch movies, or he would come along on shopping trips to the Dayton Mall with Jennie, Hether, Hill, Laura, Joey, and me.

It was on one of those shopping trips that I saw the bear. The bear was enormous and white with a blue satin bow around its neck. It cost eighty-five dollars. I saw it and immediately loved it, and that was all it took. Alex picked it up. He said, "You want it, Gorgeous, it's yours."

I said, "Oh no, it's too expensive. It's too much." But I did want it. I was already thinking how upset I'd be if I didn't get it.

He said, "Nothing's too much for you."

I said, "You shouldn't." But I was thinking, *Please get it for me. What could be more romantic?*

He kissed me and carried the bear up to the cashier. Hether, Laura, Joey, Hill, Jennie, and I watched as he pulled out his wallet and paid for the bear in cash.

Hether said, "Jesus. Someone must be getting some."

Jennie said, "Or if he's not getting some, he'd better be getting some later."

I said, "No one's getting some. He just loves me."

Joey said, "Poor frustrated bastard."

I sat in Jennie's station wagon with that bear on my lap all the way home to Richmond, Alex beside me, Laura on the other side of him, Hether and Joey in back, Hill up front next to Jennie. They were all blathering on about something, talking over one another. Alex was holding my hand, and I was holding on to the bear. Every now and then Alex would lean over and kiss me. As I sat there, the strangest feeling started coming over me, like I was in the car, but not in the car. The air felt close and hot. I rolled down my window.

My hair was blowing, but I didn't care. I was having trouble breathing. Little by little I was suffocating under-neath the bear—the bear that I had wanted so desperately less than twenty minutes earlier. The noise from all the talking was making my head hurt, and my hand was sweating where Alex was holding it, and my nose was itching from the bear's fur, and the weight of the bear was crushing the breath out of me. All I could think was, *I have got to get out of here. This bear must weigh five hundred pounds. I am going to die underneath this bear. Why can't I breathe?*

"You're so complicated, just like a series of boxes," Alex said to me sometimes, "and every time I open one, there's another inside. I don't think I'll ever get down to that last box."

How dare he try to get in my business, I wrote in my journal, the one I never kept for more than a week at a time. *Everywhere I look, he is <u>there</u>.* It was maddening, this desire of his to want to know me, to understand me, to see inside me.

I went home that night, after the trip to the mall, and I sat the great white bear in my green beanbag. I said, "You listen here, bear. You tried to kill me in that car, and don't think I don't know it. What was that about anyway?"

The bear looked at me. From my mirror, pictures of Alex, of Alex and me, smiled out into the room. They were everywhere.

I broke up with Alex a week later. I loved him, but to my mind it had to be done. I was in the prime of my life. I couldn't, wouldn't be tied down. Even as I told him good-bye, I had ideas that maybe one day we would end up together in the real world. We would have adorable curly-headed babies, some blond, some dark-haired. But that would be a long, long time from now, someday when we were very old. I would be thirty, maybe thirty-one. He would be thirty-one or thirty-two.

Earlham
College's
Barrett Hall

Older Men

I'm worried about Friday. I don't know what to wear. I don't know how to act, and most of all, I don't know how *they* will act. I only wish we could be going out with Richard (Gere) and Mikhail (Baryshnikov) instead. But we can always dream, right?

> — *Holly Ogren to Jennifer, on the eve of their*
> *first date with college boys*

Hether Rielly, Holly Ogren, Sara Ansel, and I started lurking around Earlham College second semester junior year. I was the one who first said, "I'm tired of high school boys."

Hether said, "Me too. They're so . . . high school."

I said, "Why don't we go over to Earlham and look at the boys over there?"

Holly said, "We could watch a game—soccer, lacrosse, football. That way it's not so obvious." Holly's dad worked at Earlham like mine. She was aware of the need for sneakiness.

We started going to Earlham lacrosse games. Hether drove us over and we sat in the stands and cheered on the Quakers. Richmond wasn't always tolerant of Earlham or its students. There was this overall view that Earlham kids were tree-hugging, granola-eating hippies, and a lot of them were, but we didn't mind. That semester we found them exotic. And the lacrosse players had really great legs. They didn't look like boys, either. They looked like men.

We became lacrosse groupies. We met Bill, with the hooded eyes, who Hether fell hard for. "He makes me feel like I'm in a rocket heading for the sun," she said. "Get it? He makes me hot!" We met his friend Tim, with the darkly curling hair and high cheekbones. We all swooned a bit over him, and no one was sure which of us, if anyone, he liked. We were content just being near him.

We became their friends. They looked for us at games and we hung out afterward, sometimes in the student union, sometimes in Barrett Hall, which was their dorm. They introduced us to a soccer player, Shane, who radiated a languid ease—a kind of sexy peace-love vibe that was just so *cool*. He looked like a surfer-boy hippie, tan and golden, big brown eyes, long gold-brown hair that just brushed his shoulders and fell down over his eyebrows so that he was always tossing it aside.

In Creative Writing class one day, in the midst of Mr. Dunaway's lecturing and Tommy Wissel trying to steal my shoe, Sara and Hether and I planned our futures. Sara and Tim would live in a small English Tudor home in a valley with horses, an Irish setter, and two children. Hether and Bill would own a large ranch house and have three boys and three girls (Hether came from an enormous family and was used to having lots of people around). Shane and I would live in Los Angeles in a bungalow high in the Hollywood Hills and have maybe one child (a girl) or maybe just cats.

We hung out once, the group of us, piling into Hether's car—Bill and Tim and Hether and Sara and Shane and me. Shane and I sat in the back and Hether and Sara were carrying on, being silly and stupid, acting like they were in high school. Sara was making fun of retarded people, not really meaning it, and Hether was laughing. I suddenly felt self-conscious because they sounded young. I could feel a spotlight shining down through the roof of the car on the three of us and it said, *Alert: High School Girls! High School Girls!* I thought of the bungalow in the Hollywood Hills and my face started burning.

Beside me, Shane had gone rigid. He said, "You know, my sister's retarded."

Hether and Sara went silent. Then they started backtracking. "We were just having fun." "We weren't being serious." "We would never actually make fun of retarded people."

Afterward I asked Shane if it was true. "Is your sister really retarded?"

"No," he said.

"Shane!"

"Man, I just couldn't stand the way she was talking. It wasn't cool." And then he told me, "Look, I think you're cool. I like you. But I don't like your friends. I want to hang out with you, but not with them."

So I began to go over to Earlham by myself. Sara and Hether went over a few times without me to watch some lacrosse games. Hether and Bill started dating, and not long after Sara and Holly stopped visiting Earlham altogether. I spent time with Shane on my own. He took me up to the attic of Barrett Hall, which was off limits to students, but which was where everyone who lived in Barrett Hall hung out anyway. There was old bedding up there, and a boom box that was always playing Bob Marley, UB40, and other reggae music. We climbed up there and listened to music and sat on the floor or on the big exposed pipe that ran the length of one wall, and we talked.

At first we kissed and made out a little and my head swam from Shane, from the heady mix of Barrett Attic and Earlham and older men and the exotic nature of it all. I was out of my element and we both knew it.

He put the brakes on things quickly. He told me he thought I was cool, but he needed to cut it off. I was in high school—two years younger. We were in totally different places and he was very conscious of that. If I'd been a freshman in college, he said, he would have pursued me, but in his mind I was off-limits.

At first I was disappointed, but I wanted to get to know him and I wanted to be his friend. So we hung out in Barrett Attic and talked about life. I told him I planned to be a writer and an actress in New York. These weren't things I shared with most people, especially boyfriends. But he wasn't my boyfriend. He didn't go to the high school. He didn't know any of my friends. Because the barriers were down, I felt I could tell him anything. And he listened. He took everything to heart.

Every now and then we ventured down from the attic. We went to Sunsplash at Earlham—the annual reggae festival. Afterward, someone dropped us off at my house, since

Shane didn't have a car and I didn't drive. My mom was out of town so only my dad was home. Shane was barefoot and shirtless, dressed in boxer shorts and a big floppy hat. We sat downstairs in my basement, him drunk as a skunk, me sunburned and happy from the day. We were sitting close beside each other on the couch but not doing anything. My dad came downstairs and said to Shane, "It's late. It's time to go home. Do you want a ride?"

My dad was polite but firm. It was the most polite I'd ever seen him with a boy.

Shane looked up at my dad and said, "No, sir. Thank you."

My dad stood there, waiting.

Shane got up, hat flopping, bare feet, and walked up the stairs. I followed him. Outside it was pouring rain. I said, "Dad!"

He said, "It's late," in a tone that meant no arguing.

Shane opened the front door and the rain poured down in buckets. The sky was black. He stepped out in his bare feet and boxer shorts and said "See you later" to me. And he walked off into the night.

I thought about asking Shane to the Junior-Senior Prom, but didn't. Somehow I knew he didn't belong at a high school dance. Besides, there was something about my friendship with Shane that I wanted to keep to myself, locked away in Barrett Attic. It was just for him and me, not for my friends at school to look over and dissect. There was no telling how long I would have kept hanging out there.

I showed up at the attic one day unannounced and sur-prised him with his girlfriend—a girl he'd just started see-ing. She was a college girl, unlike me. I tried to smile and laugh and act like it didn't matter, and he was cool and I was cool, and everything was *cool*. We went up to the attic once or twice after that, but I had gotten my feelings hurt. He hadn't done anything wrong. We were just friends. But I hadn't realized until that moment that I liked him so much. I couldn't get the image of him with her out of my mind. I stopped coming around.

School ended and Mom and I went to New York for the summer. I just disappeared. When I got home, the Barrett Boys and Barrett Attic were a thing of the past, nothing but a bittersweet memory.

Activities

Taking advantage of the variety of clubs offered this year, some students perfected their card skills in a friendly game; others learned more about business, geology, sports, trivia, language; others moved about taking pictures or refereeing elementary sports; and then there were those who chose not to participate in clubs but preferred using the time instead to catch up on studies, sleep, or gossip.

The newly revised speech team: Front row—Eric Ruger, Robert Ignacio, Jennifer McJunkin, Hether Rielly, Beth McDougall, Joe Kraemer, Ronnie Stier; Back row—Ross Vigran, Ian Barnes, Ned Mitchell, Danny Dickman, Tom Dehner, Larry Peterson

King and Queen of the World

Never had a speech team accomplished so much. Truly, never had human potential reached such staggering heights. For RHS, it was a proud moment.

— *1986* Pierian

In the days when the Richmond High School speech team was at its best, when we were bringing back trophies and ribbons at every meet, when each team member was a winner, we got up early for meets on Saturday mornings while all the rest of Richmond was sleeping. The dozen or so members of the team—a tired, unglamorous bunch—would assemble at school and climb yawning onto a school bus. It was still dark outside and usually cold. Mary Boots was our coach; she was a woman with a frizzy perm, a kind heart, and a talent for getting the best from us. She worked us hard. Her son Stan was copresident of the team with me. I thought he was in love with me until he invited Joey to the ballet in Ohio, and Joey said his mom wouldn't let him go because Stan meant for it to be a date.

In the dark, we set out for Rushville, Connersville, New Castle. We were the biggest school of any of them, but we never hosted meets. My old boyfriend Eric Lundquist was on the team. My mom came along sometimes, too, to chaperone and help coach.

We had a rowdy cheer we sang to wake ourselves: *Beer, beer for old Richmond High! Bring in the whiskey, bring in the rye! Send Mrs. Boots out for gin, and don't let a single sober person in! We never stumble, we never fall, We sober up on wood alcohol, When we die we'll go to Hell, we're the devils of Richmond High! Rah! Rah! Rah!*

Before each round of competition, I locked myself in a bathroom stall and did little breathing exercises my mom had taught me. I got myself so worked up before I went on that I couldn't eat, and I turned pale and even ran a fever. But once I got up in front of everyone and started performing, I loved it. Afterward, I wanted to run screaming through the halls. I was so full of myself that I couldn't be stopped.

In the poetry category, I read from Edgar Lee Masters's *Spoon River Anthology* and won almost every time. I also competed in prose, reading "The October Game" by Ray Bradbury, which was a mean little short story about a father who cuts up his daughter at a Halloween party and passes her around to the other guests in the dark. I read it very sweetly, standing up at the front of the room in my plaid skirt and corduroy blazer and lip gloss, and it was always fun to see the judges' faces when I delivered the last cruel lines. I won with that one, too.

Sophomore year, Stan and I were each awarded the highest degree possible—that of excellence from the National Forensic League, which meant that we had earned more than 250 points apiece and received the ruby insignia. It was kind of like the Academy Award for high school speech. No one at Richmond High cared very much—to them the speech team barely existed—but I knew I was a speech team rock star.

At the end of our sophomore year, Mrs. Boots told us she was moving away because her husband had been offered another job. We got a new coach—Brenda Frazier-Christie, who looked almost exactly like Mrs. Boots only black. Joey and I took it upon ourselves to hold elections for speech team president. No one ran except the two of us, who, naturally, ran together as copresidents.

In room 81, where we practiced every day after school, we gave a speech to the few remaining speech team members—the ones who hadn't abandoned ship when Mary Boots left. Mrs. Frazier-Christie wasn't there because she rarely showed up for practices.

Joey did most of the talking. I stood next to him and smiled and tried very hard to look both gracious and commanding. "As copresidents of the speech team, Jennifer and I would work for broadened publicity and individual excellence. We will always be ready to hear your proclamations or protests, or maybe just to hear your material! With good humor and dedication through and through, we hope that by strengthening the individual we will strengthen our group. And by strengthening our group we give backbone to our school. And by heartening our young, we hearten the future of America! A vote for a shared presidency is a vote for a shared future."

When Joey was finished, there was a faint round of applause, and then Jonetta Sowers-Clark said, "Who do you and Jennifer think you are, king and queen of the world?" She got up and left the room.

Joey and I looked at each other and shrugged. I thought, *Maybe we should go after her. After all, we don't have many members left.*

Joey said, "Yes?"

No one else found it funny.

By the beginning of our junior year, Brenda Frazier-Christie had left us completely. It was clear that if we still wanted Richmond High School to have a speech team, it was up to Joey and me to save it.

On a warm October day, Joey and I drove from school across the bridge by Miller's Cafeteria, past the burned-out shell of Swayne-Robinson, past the post office, down to the old train depot district where the empty warehouses and the factories were. Joey pulled into the Purina Factory lot. Up close the factory looked as tall as the Empire State Building, which was funny because from far away it didn't look very tall at all. To the right of the parking lot, there was the abandoned boxcar, just sitting there, pointed east as if it had been heading somewhere once upon a time. We climbed onto the top and sat there under the sun, looking out across the Whitewater Gorge toward the high school. We always thought best when we were somewhere we shouldn't be.

"I want a team with more interesting people," Joey said.

"Like Tom Dehner?" I said. The metal was hot under my skirt. My legs were already burning.

"Yes. That's my vision of the new speech team. You, me, and Tom Dehner."

I felt a tiny thrill in my heart—the same thrill I always felt when we discussed Tom. "But how do we get him?"

"That's the question." Joey was thinking. I could tell because he was squinting hard into the distance like he was trying to see inside each window of the high school from here.

"And can he speak, I mean, before an audience?"

"Does it matter?"

"No."

The air felt heavy and light all at once. The sun beat down. Joey's fair skin was already freckling. I tipped my head back and let the sun warm my face.

We got the best-looking teacher in the school, Mark Alexander, to agree to be our coach. Just before Christmas, an article was published in *The Register*—*Speech Team to Expand*—which mentioned that *ten of the school's top students will receive invitations to join the varsity squad*.

Then Joey and I sat down together and went through the yearbook and picked out the fifteen best people to be our new team. The first one we picked was Tom Dehner. Everyone else fell in around him. We didn't choose many girls because we didn't like them. We chose Beth McDougall because Joey liked her, and Lisa Fanning because I liked her, and Hether Rielly because she was our friend. We chose all of the good boys—except for Tom Mangas, whom I was mad at for something or other.

We called them "Speech Team Nominees" because it had a nice ring to it. We sent out letters to our chosen group informing them that the 1985/86 RHS Varsity Speech Team had been tentatively established and that *decisions concerning your membership were reached through speech interests, teacher/panel recommendations, extracurricular activities, and scholastic showmanship. You may now feel free to list Speech Team membership on college applications* . . .

Being on the speech team really wouldn't take much time, we promised. Public speaking wasn't nearly as bad or scary as classroom speaking. We added: *We have already received over 40 applications, but your spot on the Varsity Team of 15 has been secured.* Then we invited our nominees to join us on April 24 at three-fifteen p.m. for a short photo session in the library for the *Pierian. Once again, you have made no commitment, you have simply been honored for your scholastic and extracurricular aptitude. If nothing else, the pictures will get you a big spot in the yearbook and add to your momentum on the quickly arriving road to college!* Joey convinced Millie Carroll, who was the faculty sponsor in charge of yearbook photos, to send a photographer.

As part of our publicity push, Joey and I went on the local radio station with my mom and Eric Lundquist on a snowy, stormy night and talked about the new speech team. Afterward my mom drove Joey and me back to Hidden Valley to our house, and the snow was coming down so fast and white and the road was so thick with ice that we went sailing right off the road and down into a creek, screaming all the way. Luckily, the snow cushioned everything and the creek was frozen solid. We had to leave the car and climb up the hill, up to our knees in snow. We kept falling and laughing, and when we looked back, we couldn't see the car anymore. We got up to the street and walked around the corner, slipping and sliding, to my house in the blizzard, as Joey recited Robert Frost.

The woods are lovely, dark and deep . . .

The morning of the pictures, my hair, of course, didn't cooperate. It was big in all the wrong places but not big enough in all the right ones. Standing in my yellow bathroom, dressed in my favorite Esprit sundress, suffocating from Aqua Net fumes, I thought I would have a breakdown. Here it was, one of the most important days of my life, and my hair, as usual, wasn't doing what it was supposed to do. Was it too much to ask that it look good? That, just this once, it would behave? I knew that Sherri Dillon and Deanna Haskett never had these problems. They probably just jumped out of bed and their hair bounced right into perfect, perky position.

I saw Joey in AP History class, and we passed a note back and forth while Mr. Johns rattled on at the board. *We look like the ultimate Speech Presidents,* Joey said. *God, I'm soooooooooo nervous! I saw almost everyone on the new team already, but I was too scared to say anything! I have to remind Beth & Ronnie now about pictures! Good article in the paper, huh? Almost makes you think it's true, doesn't it? Almost makes you want to be a Speech Team member, doesn't it?*

I wrote back and said, *No . . . I'll never believe it. If I see it with my own eyes, then maybe—but not a second before.*

Last hour, Joey ran into Jonetta Sowers-Clark, who said, "I heard speech team photos are being taken for the yearbook after school. What time should I be there?"

Joey said, "Where did you hear that?"

She said, "Ned Mitchell was talking about it at lunch."

"Really? Did he say he was coming?"

"I don't know. So is it right after school? Why didn't you tell us? I don't think Stephanie or Michelle know. Do you want me to tell them?"

Joey said, "No. We're only taking pictures of new members now."

She gave him a suspicious look before huffing away and Joey knew it was only a matter of time before we heard from the other members, the ones who had put in so many hours in room 81 and given up so many Saturdays to make the team what it was.

Nearly everyone was in the library—and, most important, Tom Dehner was there. The new speech team members asked one or two questions about team protocol, but mostly we posed for pictures—all together—and in smaller groups by the card catalog. We were there for an hour, laughing, rearranging ourselves, smiling. The new Richmond High School speech team.

Beer, beer for old Richmond high.

Bring in the whiskey, bring in the rye . . .

And then, one by one, before we could talk about what would happen next and what our plans were for the team and its future, everyone disbanded. Tom Dehner was the first to leave. He gathered his books and grinned his crooked grin and said, "Thanks guys. I'm off."

I thought, *Where? Where?* And, *Take me with you!*

Joey and I watched him push through the turnstile, jacket and books under his arm, already heading toward the next place. Some of the others stayed around and talked.

We talked with them, but our hearts weren't in it anymore.

Joey, Hether, Ross, and I walked out to the parking lot. Hether climbed in her Cougar and Ross got into his Camaro, and Joey and I stood there waving at them till they disappeared. Then he and I jumped into the red Calais and went screaming all the way to Dayton. Joey had somehow talked Millie Carroll into giving us the negatives, and now we headed to the Dayton Mall to the one-hour developer. We were never so breathless, the music blasting, the car fly-ing, me clutching the roll of film in my hand. We talked and laughed, and pulled up to the mall in what seemed at once like minutes and hours, and tumbled out and started running.

"These are very important pictures," we told the man behind the One-Hour Moto Photo counter, who looked bored and ready to go home for the day.

"Okay," he said.

"No," I said. "You don't understand. These are the most important pictures you will ever develop. Please be *very, very, very* careful."

His eyes got wide. "Okay," he said. He seemed a little scared of us. He looked at the negatives. "Since these were shot in black and white, I can print them in either black and white or sepia. That's with a brown tint. So it looks kind of old-fashioned."

We said at the same time, "Sepia."

After he promised to have them done in an hour, we milled about and bought hot pretzels and an Orange Julius each and sat and ate.

"I can't believe they showed up," said Joey. "That *Tom Dehner* showed up."

"I know," I said. I sighed a little. "Did it really happen?"

"I don't know. We'll see when the pictures come back."

"What if the pictures come back blank?" I said.

We shivered. We ate.

I said, "What do you think will happen to the team?"

Joey said, "As long as those pictures come back fine, who cares?"

When the hour was up, we went back to the photo place and stood at the counter, waiting. The man brought us our pictures and asked if we wanted to check them first before we walked away, and we told him no, we wanted to sit down and enjoy them.

We chose a bench that was quiet and away from the crowd and sat down side by side. We opened the envelope. We were very quiet. We pulled them out of the sleeve. At the same time, we caught our breath. They were more wonderful than we'd imagined. It was maybe our greatest success so far.

Here was one of all of us together. And another. Another. Another. Ned Mitchell with his fist in the air, his arm around Robert Ignacio. Danny Dickman, Ian Barnes, Eric Ruger, Ross, and me. Joey, Hether, Ronnie Stier, Robert, Ned, and me with Tom Dehner. The entire group of us milling around, unposed, laughing. Joey and me, just the two of us, leaning on the card catalog, grinning like two Cheshire cats. Tom Dehner leaving the library, pushing through the turnstile, his books and jacket under his arm, on his way to somewhere . . .

When we got all the way through to the end, we went back and began to talk over them, choosing our favorites, analyzing this one and that one. We sat there for nearly an hour, lost in the moment.

The speech team fell apart after that. None of the new

members ever came to meetings or practices. They didn't show up for meets. Mr. Alexander abandoned us. One by one, the original members of the team disappeared. We saw them in the halls of school and some of them smiled and waved, and some of them looked away. But we still had our pictures, which we got out from time to time and looked at, of the speech team that might have been, that almost was, that still existed, just for a moment, on film.

The Richmond High School History Team. From left to right: Ronnie Stier, Joe Kraemer, Jennifer McJunkin, Holly Ogren, and Eric Ruger

Triumphs and Tragedies

It was hard working as a group at first. We're all very different people. But then everything came together somehow—the ideas, the research, us—and before we knew it, we were a team.

—*Jennifer, interviewed in the* Palladium-Item, *April 1, 1985*

When we were still in the midst of planning the new speech team, Joey and I drove down to the Purina Factory and this time we walked past our favorite boxcar. We climbed instead up the narrow metal ladder on the side of the Purina tower, the one that stretched toward the sky, careful not to let anyone see us. This was something we usually did only at night. I looked only up, not down, as I climbed, till we got to the very top, up where the Christmas tree sat year-round slightly tilted. We stood for a moment before sitting down in the sun. From up here you could see all of Richmond.

We were well into the fall of our junior year and time was running out. If we were ever going to get Tom Dehner, we needed to figure something out now.

This time I was the one who thought of the plan. I said, "What about a history team?" We sat facing the high school.

Joey said, "What's a history team?"

I said, "It's something that sounds really nerdy, but is actually only slightly nerdy. You get to wear costumes and perform in front of people and have them clap for you and win awards. I did it twice in junior high. I won district and state both times, and got to go to nationals in Washington, D.C."

"Washington?" Joey sat up straight. I could tell his mind was already spinning with images of him, me, and Tom Dehner in D.C.

"You can have as many as five to a group."

Much like with the speech team, we considered the candidates carefully. More carefully this time because there was an actual competition involved and I wanted to win. We both did. We needed people who could help us do that. They had to be smart, capable, and, if possible, comfortable in front of an audience.

We both agreed Holly Ogren fit the criteria. She was in our AP History class, a good student, and as responsible as a parent. She was also used to performing because she sang not only in concert choir but in Madrigals and sometimes appeared in Drama Club productions.

The next day at school, we asked Holly if she would be interested and she said yes. Then Joey wrote a note to

Ronnie Stier, who was also in our History class. Ronnie was good-looking and smart, a super-cool jock. We were sort-of friends with him, but asking him to be on the history team was something else. Ronnie and Tom were very good friends. We couldn't approach Tom Dehner till we found out Ronnie's decision. Getting Tom depended on getting Ronnie.

Ronnie said he'd think about it. For days we lived on pins and needles. Would he do it? He was a football player. Why would he be interested in a history team? Finally, on a Monday morning, after an endless weekend of waiting and wondering, I wrote Ronnie a note in AP History and passed it back to him.

R., Have you thought about it? Write back this time because I want to know what you think. Jennifer

After about a hundred years, the piece of paper came back to me. It said: *I'll do it.*

We got Ronnie to ask Tom Dehner, and, miracle of miracles, Tom said yes. *Yes!* The Richmond High School History Team was complete.

One snowy day, we all met at my house. Joey arrived first and then Holly. We ran from window to window screaming—even responsible, rational Holly—until we saw Ronnie's red car pull up in front. Tom and Ronnie got out and came up the walk, wearing their letter jackets. They kind of ambled, hands shoved in jean pockets to ward off the cold, as if they had all the time in the world to get to the front door. Out on my front lawn, the red and gray of their letter jackets standing out against all that white, they glimmered almost a little above perfect.

Inside, Tom sat on the long, low sofa by Joey's chair, and I sat next to Tom. Ronnie sat in a chair across from Joey. Holly was on the piano bench. I thanked God we had a cool house with cool artwork, even if we did live on the wrong side of town. My parents may have lacked good real estate sense, but they did have taste.

We talked about the parameters and themes of this year's contest: Triumphs and Tragedies in History. We tossed out possible ideas. All of mine were based on costumes I might like to wear (a hoop skirt, a flapper's dress, a pencil skirt and pumps like Bonnie Parker) or stories that I was fascinated by (Leopold and Loeb, Bonnie and Clyde, Jesse James). Joey's wit was sharp and on target. I did my best to both shimmer and not be too silly. Holly didn't talk and we were thankful. Ronnie was sweet and cute. Tom was easy, warm, and funny—completely himself. He was sitting on my couch— *my* couch!

Hours later, after Tom and Ronnie left, we weren't any nearer to figuring out what the subject of our performance should be—maybe something on the Civil War? No event in American history seemed more dramatic or complicated or more tragic. Reconstruction could be considered a triumph in many ways. Plus, I loved Scarlett O'Hara.

After Holly left, Joey stayed. I moved over onto the very spot where Tom Dehner had sat. It was still warm. "Oh," I said. "Tom Dehner sat here . . ."

"Let me have a turn," Joey said.

"Not yet," I said. "Just a minute longer."

For days afterward, Joey and I talked about the meeting. Had Tom Dehner really been at my house? Had he sat on my sofa? Was he really and truly on the history team?

One week later, we presented everyone with the schedule of district, state, and nationals—when each competition would occur, should we advance, so that everyone could write it on their calendars. Tom not only played football, he also played baseball, which was one of the many reasons we loved him. He could, it was clear, do anything.

As soon as he saw the schedule, Tom came to us and said he had a problem. "I can't do the history team. My baseball schedule conflicts with state and nationals."

Joey said, "We don't even know that we're going to get to state or nationals."

Tom said, "But what if we do? I can't hold us back. We haven't even picked a topic. It's better that you guys get someone else now before we even get started."

We couldn't believe it. We had been so close and now, just like that, he was gone.

We had to decide what to do. Forget about the whole idea, tell Ronnie and Holly we weren't going to do it, or move on with someone else.

Holly said, "I still want to do it."

Ronnie said, "I'm still in. But who are we going to get?"

We went round and round about it. *How do you replace Tom Dehner?* Finally, we decided on Eric Ruger. He was a good friend of Ronnie's—quiet, good-looking. He threw fun parties on his farm. He was a wild card because we didn't know if he could perform in front of an audience or if he was even a good history student, but we liked him. The most important thing was he was someone we could all agree on.

We based our play on a private collection of letters to and from W. G. Eaton, agent for the Bureau of Refugees, Freedmen and Abandoned Lands in Georgia and South Carolina from 1865 to 1866. A friend of my mom and dad's had given them the letters, knowing how much they both loved history. We decided that so many of the human problems of Reconstruction in the South had passed through the Freedmen's bureau offices, and we tried to show a slice of life by dramatizing just such an hour in W. G. Eaton's workday.

Ronnie played W. G. Eaton. Holly was Emily, a northern schoolteacher who was in the South to teach black children. Eric was Robert, owner of Mulberry Plantation, who came to the Freedmen's bureau to hire freed slaves to work his fields. I was Margaret, a southern plantation owner widowed in the war and resentful of the North. Joey played a college student (and our narrator) just returned from presenting a paper he wrote about the era of Reconstruction.

We ended the play with Lincoln's Second Inaugural Address: "With malice toward none; with charity for all; with firmness in the right, as God gives us to see the right, let us strive on to finish the work we are in . . ." My mom, who served as our coach, helped us sort through the research and draft our ten-minute play, which we called *Malice, Charity, and the Children of Pride: The Reconstruction of the South*. Mr. Johns, our AP History teacher, became our faculty sponsor.

In April, we won the district competition. The *Palladium-Item* covered the story, saying: *The group chose the Reconstruction for two reasons. After reading* Gone With the Wind, *McJunkin said, she always wanted to wear a hoop skirt and this would give her the perfect opportunity. Second, the topic fit in well with the theme of the competition—"Triumphs and Tragedies in History."*

My mom said, "Mercy, Jennifer, why did you say that about the hoop skirt?"

"Because it's true."

"But it makes your whole reason for wanting to do a project on the Civil War sound so frivolous."

"But it's true," I said. I thought it made me sound funny

and flirty. "I do want to wear a hoop skirt. That's one of the main reasons we chose Reconstruction."

I got to wear a wonderful costume—all of our costumes except for Joey's (his own jacket and tie) and Ronnie's (an actual Union officer's uniform from the actual Civil War) came from the Earlham College costume department. Besides my hoop skirt I had a wide hat with streamers that looked like something Vivien Leigh might have worn. As the northern schoolteacher, Holly's plain blue dress and cro-cheted shawl were dumpy and frumpy, and Eric's suspend-ers and black hat made him look like a member of Duran Duran.

May 10 and 11, just days before my birthday, we headed to Indiana University in Bloomington for the state finals. At IU, we stayed in the dorms with the other contestants. The night before our presentation, the five of us broke into the theater where we'd be performing and chased one another in the dark wings of the stage. Afterward, we came out into the lobby into a crowd of people dressed up for a prom. There was a fat girl in an ugly dress who was loud and obnoxious. Joey or Ronnie insulted her and her boyfriend started a fight. Ronnie was given a black eye, which Joey explained, in an impromptu way during our performance the next day, was a result of a bad scene in the Civil War. I stepped out of character and said, "I love a man who can stand being hit. I think it's courageous."

We won first place. We were going to nationals. The *Palladium-Item* wrote, *Jennifer McJunkin's prediction came true. She said five weeks ago that the five members of the Richmond High School history team would win the state contest—and they did—Saturday in the Indiana University auditorium. Now she will get to wear her hoop skirt again.*

• • •

Even Ronnie seemed excited about D.C. He had remained wildly unmoved through district and state, but he wasn't nearly as Steve McQueen–cool over nationals. Almost everyone went with us June 11–14 to the University of Maryland, where the competition was held—our teacher Mr. Johns, Mr. and Mrs. Kraemer and Joey's brothers Mitchell and Matthew, Mr. and Mrs. Ruger, Mrs. Stier, and my mom.

Our families stayed in hotels while the five of us lived in one of the dorms at the University of Maryland with all the other History Day participants. We were separated by the elevators—the boys on one side of the hall, girls on the other. Holly and I had a huge, spacious room with wide windows, large enough for ten people. We had never felt so free.

On the afternoon of Thursday, June 13, we competed on stage in front of other groups and an audience of people from all over the country. It was our best performance to date—we all knew it and felt it. After it was over we were flushed and excited and jumpy. Strangers came up to congratulate us and tell us how much they loved us and our presentation. "We won," I said. "I know we won."

Not long after, we were called back into the auditorium to hear the results: the announcement of the six groups to make it to the final round. We sat side by side in the audience, surrounded by our families and our teacher, and waited for our names to be called. But when the list was read, six other groups were chosen. They didn't call our names. We couldn't believe it. We hadn't won. *We hadn't even made it to the finals*. We sat there deflated while people approached us and said, "What happened?" "You were the best." "The judges are crazy." "Don't give up. You guys can win next year."

We were allowed to pick up our scores in the judges' room. Eric and I went with my mom while the others waited outside. Inside, the room was a mob scene as coaches and teachers and students fought their way through, holding manila envelopes, reading over judges' comments and scores. My mom was handed ours and passed it back to me. Eric followed her out of the room, staying close. I opened the envelope and pulled out our tally sheet, grabbing on to the back of Eric's shirt so I wouldn't get left behind.

Judge one—98.
Judge two—99.
Judge three—97.
Average score—94.

"The numbers are wrong!" I was yanking on Eric's shirt.

"What?" It was too loud. He couldn't hear me. I held the sheet in front of his face and pointed.

"They added wrong! Our average was ninety-eight, not ninety-four. Tell Mom. Get my mom!"

Eric started reaching for my mom. "Mrs. McJunkin!"

We stumbled outside into the hall after her. She said, "What is it?"

We showed her. She went white and then red. Then she moved into action. She found Mr. Johns. Together they went to every official, every representative, every judge they could find for the 1985 National History Day. While they did this, Eric and I found the others and told them what happened. Surely they would fix this. It was their mistake, not ours. The final round hadn't happened yet. There was still time. We could still compete and win.

My mother and Mr. Johns were passed from one person to another to another to another until they were finally handed over to the national director of National History Day, Dr. Sharon Lutz. She was a small, defensive woman with white-blond hair and black glasses and a sharp bird's face. The five of us—Joey, Eric, Holly, Ronnie, and I—went with them to meet her. Mom and Mr. Johns explained what had happened. They showed her the judges' scores and the miscalculation that had been made.

Dr. Lutz said, "What do you expect me to do about it?"

My mother, in her most gracious tone, said, "We're hoping that you will include them in the final round and not punish them for an error they didn't make."

Dr. Lutz said, "It's too late. We've already made the announcement." And then she looked at us. "It's time these children learned that life isn't always fair. Life is just a poker game. They'll get over it."

We stood there staring at her. She was the first truly horrible person Joey, Holly, Ronnie, Eric, and I had ever met, with her cold voice and her pinched bird face. She looked at my mom again, impatient.

My mother then gave Dr. Lutz a southern-lady piece of her mind. Mr. Johns—usually so reticent, so happy to be in the background—stepped in and joined her. But Dr. Lutz was unyielding. There was nothing she would do.

It was the first time we cried as friends. We hugged one another and held on together, all in a group. Ronnie swore and punched a metal trash can and nearly broke his hand. Joey ran away to an empty stadium, surrounded by empty bleachers, and cried a part of his heart out. Holly and I walked and walked all over campus, arm in arm. We cried and looked at the stars, and every now and then we saw an angry blur run by and it was Eric or Ronnie.

• • •

Back at the dorm, the disappointment of the day caught up with us. Mitchell Kraemer stayed with us as we lassoed people with a rope in the hall and spent the evening screaming up and down the halls. We played hide and seek. We arranged our history team set inside the elevator, complete with all our antique props, the ones we were so proud of. I put on my hoop dress and Ronnie put on his Yankee blue uniform, and every time the door opened the five of us stood there in full Civil War attire, welcoming people to our reduced but marvelous Confederate world of 1866.

When we got tired of this, we went back to the boys' room and talked about what had happened to us. Eric cried then for the first time, sitting on his bed, leaning against the wall. I was across the room from him at the foot of Ronnie's bed next to Ronnie. Joey was next to Eric. Holly was sprawled on a chair, Mitchell on the floor. As Eric was talking, Joey pulled out a toy gun that belonged to his little brother Matthew, who was seven, and pointed it at Eric who jumped about twenty-five feet into the air. "You asshole," he said when he could talk again. But we were laughing, which felt good.

"Let's go to D.C.," said Ronnie.

So at two in the morning, the five of us, with Mitchell, got into Ronnie's car and drove downtown to the Lincoln Memorial. Together we climbed the steps and stood in front of Abraham Lincoln, the true inspiration for our play. Then we stood looking up at the very words we had spoken. *With malice toward none; with charity for all* . . . We read the words out loud just as we had read them in our performance, saying the last lines together.

I pulled out my camera and gave it to Mitchell. Joey, Holly, Ronnie, Eric, and I stood underneath the words of

Lincoln's Second Inaugural Address. We posed for a photo and then the five of us stood once more in front of Abraham Lincoln. We stood there a long time, and after promising we would be friends forever, we headed back down the steps.

We knew that we didn't have it in us to re-form the team senior year and come up with another project. Several weeks after we returned from Maryland, National History Day officials wrote us to say that the history team would be receiving national medals in a special ceremony in Indiana and official letters of regret. They would also be paying special attention to their scoring methods and reevaluating those methods, based on what had happened to us. For us, it was small compensation for the loss we'd endured.

But there was so much we had gained. We were different, diverse, but we had come together and worked together and were disappointed together and had our hearts broken together. After a while we forgot that Tom Dehner was ever on the team. It seemed like Eric had always been there, from the very start.

After it was all over, Ronnie wrote me a letter. I was in New York City for the summer with my mom.

July 11, 1985: I haven't thought a whole lot about the History Team lately. Then every once in a while somebody will tell me how bad it was that we lost. Even people I don't know. It's kind of a funny feeling. I hope this letter gets to you before you leave the Big Apple. Friends Forever. Love, Ronnie.

The Richmond State Hospital

Community Outreach

No smoking, loud talking, spitting on the floors or stoves will be tolerated.

—General Rules of St. Stephen's Hospital, Richmond, Indiana, 1884

Christmastime in Richmond meant several things: snow days, freezing temperatures, the live manger scene at First Methodist Church on National Road West, Christmas lights and decorations on the downtown Promenade, our dog Tosh howling along with the piano as my mom played our favorite Christmas carols, and long lists to my grandparents detailing every single thing I wanted (posters of Duran Duran, Cheap Trick, and Rick Springfield; T-shirts with cute sayings on them; Esprit clothes; new record albums from all my favorite bands . . .). It also meant Lois Potts's annual

Quaker Christmas project for the community. This was when Lois Potts—my former Girl Scout leader, the same Lois Potts who had chosen me to play the Virgin Mary and her daughter Kimberly to be Joseph in the yearly Christmas pageant the first year I lived in Richmond—organized members of Clear Creek Friends Meeting to visit the sick at Reid Memorial Hospital or sing carols to shut-ins or take the old people who lived at Golden Rule Nursing Center on a field trip to Richmond Square Mall.

In December 1985, Lois Potts announced that she was going to take her Christmas cheer to the Richmond State Hospital, which, until 1927, had been known as the Eastern Indiana Hospital for the Insane. We were all terrified of the Richmond State Hospital and the people who lived there—crazy people, mentally disabled people, violent people of all ages. There were even criminals who were too wicked and wild to be kept in the tiny Wayne County Jail downtown across from the Courthouse. Growing up, my friends and I lived in fear of someone escaping. Heather Craig lived near the hospital and I was almost too scared to spend the night at her house. Whenever we heard a strange noise outside, we were sure it was an escaped mental patient walking on the roof or hiding in the bushes.

When Lois Potts announced she was going to the State Hospital to sing carols and take presents, no one—adults or kids—wanted to go with her. Finally, my mother, who was both practical and kindhearted, said that she would go. She was one of the few people I knew who was not afraid of the Richmond State Hospital or the people who lived there. My father was busy, of course, but my mother would take me along. And Joey, because he was my best friend (even though he was Catholic and not Quaker), would go, too.

To prepare, my mother chose some of her favorite carols, and Joey and I practiced a dramatic reading of 'Twas the Night Before Christmas, which we were going to deliver speech-team style, as we had many a scene from a play, in a kind of duet.

So it was that four days before Christmas break, the four of us met in the main building of the Richmond State Hospital: Lois Potts (mid-forties—dark short-cropped hair, black-rimmed glasses, no-nonsense manner, resembling a great overbearing string bean); my mother (early forties—slim, blue-eyed, black-haired, pretty, wearing some sort of mid-1980s outfit befitting a Richmond housewife); Joey (eighteen—blond, glasses, pretty); me (seventeen—brunette, pretty, and boy crazy as could be).

We were not alone. This was ward-party day at the hospital. There were Santa Clauses of various shapes and ages, and bags of gifts (two each for every patient in the twenty-three wards) and holiday goodies and punch. The Old National Road Chapter of Sweet Adelines, a women's barbershop singing group, was there to perform songs for one of the women's wards. Volunteers were there from the Eastern Gateway Kiwanis Club and Home Bible Study of Adams County, as well as West Richmond Friends Meeting, which was not to be confused with us. West Richmond Friends had been coming to the hospital at Christmastime for years, ever since a man named Orval Fetters started the tradition.

A luncheon was prepared for all of the volunteers by Frances Lippke of the hospital's dietary department, and then we were sent out to spread Christmas cheer to the crazy people.

When it came time for our particular ward assignment, one of the guards signed us in and said, "Now I'll escort you to the maximum security building."

Lois Potts, whose arms were filled with bags of wrapped presents, didn't bat an eye. My mother, whose arms were also filled with bags of wrapped presents, said, "Excuse me?"

The guard said, "It's one of our Acute Intensive Treatment Wards. We keep them in a separate building because of security risks. We have to with the eighteen- to thirty-five-year-old maximum security male inmates. A lot of 'em are violent or dangerous to themselves or others. But don't worry. We'll have a guard with you at all times. If anything happens, we'll get you out of there."

My mother and Joey and I stood there, staring at the guard, staring at one another. Lois Potts said, "Lead the way."

The maximum security building was barred up and locked tight as any prison, and I knew about prisons because I had a fascination with them that went back to childhood, so much so that, at the age of nine, I had created a prison mystery series in the vein of the Nancy Drew stories: *Debby, who was the prettiest of the group, was full of mysteries and puzzles. She sang and danced in nightclubs and spent her time at home reading. Debby turned into the driveway which led to Sandsky Prison. She parked the car and climbed out. "Ah, smell that fresh air!" she said, spreading her arms far apart.*

My parents weren't sure where this fascination came from—it was just one of those mysterious, unexplainable interests of mine, like my unreasonable love and affinity for Jesse James, Sweden, tambourines, and Kraft Macaroni & Cheese.

The maximum security ward looked a lot like a prison, so much so that a tiny part of me did a thrilling little jump as the guard let us in.

The inmates, as they called them, were very happy to

see us. These were men, black and white, big and strong, tall and short, broad and skinny—but most of them big and strong and broad—who, as my mom said later, looked as if they had not seen a female in years. They remained happy— and friendly, and surprisingly well-behaved—throughout the singing of Christmas carols (Lois Potts banging away at the piano), the opening of presents, and the eating and drinking of refreshments.

At one point I went into the kitchen to look for some more paper cups, and a boy followed me in there. He was maybe a couple years older than I, with feathered blond hair that was also a little wavy. He had dark eyes and he was good-looking in a bad news kind of way. He shambled when he walked and had an air about him like he had been hor- ribly wounded and hurt by someone somewhere down the line. He reminded me of Matt Dillon in *Rumble Fish*.

"Hey," he said. He kind of slumped against the counter.

"Hey."

"You got any cigarettes?"

"No."

He shrugged, and then he smiled and it was wicked and sweet all at once, and I thought, *Uh-oh*.

He said, "What's your name?"

I said, "Jennifer," wondering if I should have told him my real name, if maybe now he might break out one night and come find me. He was, after all, a patient in the eighteen- to thirty-five-year-old maximum security all-male ward at the state mental health facility.

He said, "I'm Andy. What year are you?"

"Senior."

He nodded. "I was a senior when they busted me."

Thrillthrillthrill. "What did they bust you for?"

"Drugs. I was stupid. And now I'm here getting clean."

It was the same little thrill I felt when I looked at the cover of Cheap Trick's *Heaven Tonight,* at Tom Petersson's bloodshot eyes, and imagined all the wicked and unspeakable things he had done even minutes before the picture was snapped—smoking, drinking, having sex, maybe even taking drugs.

Andy said, "Maybe I could call you sometime."

I was trying to picture him calling and my dad answering in one of his many foreign accents. "Do they ever let you out of here?" I said. Where would we go? I tried to imagine us at a football game or at Noble Roman's or Clara's or at Rip's house for a party. Would I have to drive? Was he allowed to drive? Did he even have a license?

"No, but I don't have much longer. I'd like to take you out."

At that moment, my mother, who had an uncanny ability to sense when I was about to make a horrible decision or endanger my life, appeared. "I found some cups in the other room," she said, smiling tightly at both of us. "Jennifer, why don't you come help me pour?"

After refreshments, Joey and I performed our dramatic reading of *'Twas the Night Before Christmas.* The men were surprisingly attentive while we read—standing in front of them, side by side, the book open before us, alternating lines. At one point, two or three of the men started getting a little restless, whispering to each other and talking over us. We kept reading:

Joey: "When out on the lawn there arose such a clatter . . ."

Jennifer: "I arose from my bed to see what was the
matter . . ."

The men kept talking, so we just spoke a little louder to
be heard above them.

Joey: "When, what to my wondering eyes should
appear . . ."
Jennifer: "But a miniature sleigh, and eight tiny rein-
deer . . ."

Finally, one of the men—a great big, burly man with a
head as bald and shiny as a melon and tattoos up and down
both arms—stood up and shouted, *Shut up, goddammit! I
want to hear the story!*" The talking men stared at him and
fell silent. We all stared at him. Joey and I didn't say a word
until he waved us on. "Keep reading," he said. "I want to
hear the rest of it." And he sat back down.

We kept reading, and for the rest of the story everyone
was quiet.

We should have stopped there, of course. It would have
been a perfect way to end the evening. Everyone was sleepy
and settled and somewhat content. My mom and Joey and
I were more than ready to leave. But Lois Potts had one
more activity planned. Square dancing. I will never understand why she thought this could possibly be a good thing to
do with eighteen- to thirty-five-year-old maximum security
male inmates at a mental hospital, but she was very cheer-
ful as she said, "I want everyone to join me in the Virginia
Reel."

It's hard to know who was more shocked: my mother,
Joey, me, or the men, who began stomping and whistling.

You'd have thought she had introduced a stripper out of a
cake or that she'd just passed around a box of *Playboys*. I'd
never seen a group of people so excited about square dancing.

"Now let's choose our partners," she said.

"I want that one!" one of them shouted, pointing at me.
My mother moved in front of me, standing between me and
them.

"I'll take that one," another yelled, pointing at my
mother.

"Well, I'll have that one," screamed the bald man, pointing right at Joey. No one wanted Lois Potts.

We paired up, standing across from our partners in two
lines, most of the men forced to dance with each other, and
Lois Potts explained that there would be no touching in this
version of the Virginia Reel because we were leaving out
the twirl. (Lois explained later that she thought it would be
"overstimulating" for the inmates.) Then she lowered a nee-
dle on the record she had brought with her, unbeknownst
to my mother and Joey and me, just for this purpose. Over
the sounds of fiddles and banjo, we met our partners in the
middle and began to promenade and do-si-do—something I
had learned in gym class back in the fourth grade.

The men were very enthusiastic, especially Joey's partner, the big, bald tattooed man who had so loved *'Twas
the Night Before Christmas*. He kept hollering along with
the music, making up his own square dancing calls, which
sounded more like the hog calling you heard at the local
fair. I was looking everywhere for Andy, but he was nowhere
to be seen and I wondered vaguely, as I was being jolted
this way and that, if he had managed to escape. My partner
seemed to be the leader of the inmates—a tall, lean black
guy who looked almost exactly like Officer Bobby Hill on

Hill Street Blues, only without the smile. My mother's partner kept trying to hold her close, even though there was
supposed to be no touching.

When it came time for the twirl—when we reached
that point in the dance where the twirl should have been,
and we didn't twirl—my partner, the leader, stopped dancing and said, "I want to twirl." He just stopped right in the
middle of everyone, men bumping into him left and right,
and stared right at Lois Potts with a look that said No One
Has Ever Refused Me Anything and Lived to Tell the Tale.

She said, "I don't think we'd better."

He said, "I want to twirl," and he said it very, very firmly,
so that you could imagine what he might have done on The
Outside to get himself in here, in a facility where we were,
after all, locked in behind bars.

They stood staring at each other for what seemed like
twenty minutes or so, like the final showdown scene out of
a western, before Lois Potts finally said, "Let's do the twirl,"
as if she had thought of it all on her own. The men clapped
and cheered, and Lois began the record over. I looked at
my mother and Joey. Their faces were flushed. Their hair
was messy. Joey's glasses were askew. I thought, *Dear Jesus,
if you can hear me. You got us into this mess in the first place, if
you want to be technical about it. We wouldn't even be here if it
weren't for you. The least you can do is get us out of here alive.*

The dance eventually ended and we gathered our things.
We bundled ourselves up in our layers of coats and scarves
and gloves and hats and then the guard escorted us out into
the winter night. As we walked to our cars, we could still
hear the sounds of the men clapping and cheering and singing "Turkey in the Straw."

Laura Lonigro, Joey Kraemer, and Jennifer McJunkin
from their *Judy on Purpose* photo shoot

Experimental Writers Group

Joey and I were talking on the phone last night, and we pondered on a terrible thought—all we talk about and think about now is Tom Dehner—what if he died? We would have nothing to live for, to fight for, to talk about, to dream of!

—*Jennifer to Holly Ogren, AP History class*

Joey and I thought up *Judy on Purpose* with Laura Lonigro on the back porch of Laura's house at the end of summer 1985. Over a bowl of macaroni, we made up our minds to write a play that would make us famous in the world outside Richmond and would also make us famous in the halls of Richmond High School. We planned to cast Tom Dehner in one of the leading roles. Laura loved him as much as Joey and I did, and it was, we decided, the perfect way to get him, once and for all.

We met almost every day from the middle of July until school started, on the porch of Laura's house. Her parents were separated and her mother had just moved to Dayton, leaving Laura and her sister Monica alone with their dad, who was suddenly staying away from home more and more. We had the run of the house.

The three of us had very different working styles. "You couldn't put three more different people together," Joey said to us one day that summer.

He was pacing and talking—and talking and talking without stopping for breath. Laura and I were mostly listening. Laura was smoking cigarette after cigarette and swearing at mosquitoes. I was writing my name in purple ink on my notebook and trying to decide if I liked my toenail polish.

Joey stopped and pointed at me. "Jennifer, so pretty and girly and flirty and sensual, writing everything in purple pen."

He pointed at Laura. "Laura, so loud and Italian and messy and sexy, with those cigarettes and those hand-scrawled pages flying everywhere."

He took her cigarette from her and inhaled. "And me, so shrill and uptight—funny, but wicked, and with a real mean streak, trying like a lunatic to organize this shit."

I was writing *Jennifer loves Matt Ashton* over and over. Then I wrote *Jennifer & Matt. Jennifer Ashton*. Matt and I were still writing to each other all the time and seeing each other when we could on school breaks and holidays.

Laura looked at me and said, "Uptight? Joey? What the fuck's he talking about? Oh my God. I would never call him uptight. Shrill maybe. Uptight? I don't know, man." She started laughing.

I was looking at Joey. I said, "Sensual? Why am I sensual and not sexy?"

Laura said, "Hey. Yeah. I'd rather be sensual. Sexy makes me sound like a harlot."

Joey sat down on the edge of the porch and rolled his eyes. He kept her cigarette, crushing it out with his foot. He said, "We are never going to get anything written."

We decided our play would be called *Judy on Purpose*. It would be about a girl named Judy Diamond, the girl next door, who was hapless and sweet, but who bad things happened to all the time even though she was very well meaning and good-hearted. The story would center on Judy and her struggles to live a somewhat normal life in a crazy, mixed-up world, which the three of us felt we could relate to. Judy would have a funny, awful, dysfunctional family, one that drove her to distraction and ruined her life, sometimes on purpose, sometimes by accident.

She would have a sister Lolita who believed herself to be Margaret Thatcher (and who would walk around singing "God save our gracious Queen, Long live our noble Queen!"), an adopted brother named Rock (cynical and sarcastic and sometimes suicidal—no one in the family was sure where he came from or how he came to be there), Rock's slut of a girlfriend Sharon (who was a fixture in the house), and Mother Diamond (le grand dame), who we decided would manufacture spotlights because it seemed like the most outlandish thing we could think of. Even before we knew the beginning or the middle of the play, we knew it would end with Judy in a clothing store choosing between an Izod, a Fox, and a no-brand-name shirt. It was to be very deep and profound.

After we briefly outlined the story and characters, we jumped to the most interesting part of the process—casting. Laura, who had acted in and worked on nearly every production ever to hit McGuire Hall, wanted to play Lolita Diamond. Joey wasn't interested in acting. He did, however, want to direct. We all decided I would be Judy.

That left the other parts. We pulled out the yearbook and went to town. We cast Holly Ogren as Mother Diamond because she had a certain overly bright quality that we thought suited the role. Jeff Shirazi would be adopted brother Rock Diamond because he had black hair like Laura and was smart enough to understand cynicism. Our friend Diane Armiger was Sharon (the "live-in slut") because of her platinum hair color. A junior named Kelly Shepard was Father Douglas (the priest) because he was a good actor and had what we thought to be a very ironic yet understanding smile. Tom Dehner, of course, was Michael, the date, the boy who sweeps Judy off her feet—or tries to in spite of herself and her insane family.

"Do you think Tom Dehner can act?" Laura said.

"No," I said.

"But does it matter?" Joey said.

"No," we all said together.

Our target date for finishing was September 21. When we didn't make that deadline, we aimed for Thanksgiving. When we weren't done by then, we planned for Christmas.

We made detailed schedules for ourselves—scene breakdowns, deadlines. We met after school, during school, instead of school, and on weekends. Joey typed up the schedules for us. *It will be done Christmas Eve, 1985, or that's it,* he wrote. *Meeting times: Fridays at 3:15, various weekend dates. We've got to be willing to give up some weekends, even nights (now that football is over) to get this done!! I'm not kidding!! We have to have goals and rules in order to obtain them! Let's sacrifice, got that, Laura!!! And no dates either, Jennifer. I'll even fork over the cigarettes, what the hell.*

Part of the problem was that each of us had a lot to say and we loved to hear ourselves talk. And we didn't completely sacrifice our social lives because we were focused on parties with a whole new intensity.

But we were also dedicated. Joey and I had a meeting with Mr. Sizemore, head of the theater department, about getting our play produced. The Drama Club was known for its annual shows in McGuire Hall. *You Can't Take It With You, Annie, The Miracle Worker, The Sound of Music. Judy on Purpose* would be different from anything that had ever hit the RHS stage, but Mr. Sizemore seemed impressed and said he would take a look at it as soon as we could get it to him, that he would consider it for spring production.

That was when we got down to business. First and foremost, we decided to take some time off from school so we could work on the play. Because I was the conscientious one in the group, I made the mistake of asking permission the first time we took a "creative day," as we called them. It was Thursday, November 21, 1985. My mother was getting ready to go on a research trip for her book on Carl Sandburg. She would be gone just a few days, and I wanted to take Friday off. My father would stay with me, working too much as always, running on the weekend, cooking, listening to his music, smoking his pipe. The three of us, once so inseparable, moving as a unit, now moved in our own distinct worlds more and more—my mom consumed by her book and her research, my father with Earlham-Earlham-Earlham, me with my friends, my play, boys, parties.

Mom was in my parents' room packing. I lurked about in the doorway, waiting for her to notice me.

She said, "Yes?"

I said, "Are you excited about your trip?"

She said, "I'm looking forward to it."

I asked her some questions about where she was going and the people she would see so that she knew I was interested and making an effort to be involved, and then she said, "Was there something you wanted to ask me?" My mother had these invisible antennae that could pick up on the littlest thing. It was spooky and unnerving.

"Well, you know how Joey and Laura and I are working on *Judy on Purpose*, and we've already talked to Mr. Sizemore and he said he would consider it for spring production if we can just get it to him on time, but there is never any time to work on it because we are always having to be in school."

"No," she said. She was folding up her shirts and pants in neat little rows.

"I haven't even asked you yet."

"You can't skip school on Friday to work on your play."

My mother was like an alien being with her ability to read minds. I was suddenly mad at myself for even asking her for permission. Who did that? Who asked their mother for permission to ditch school? I thought I deserved points for this.

"At least I asked you," I said. "I could have just ditched, but I wanted to do it the right way."

She stopped folding and looked at me with her most patient impatient look.

My mother left the next day and my dad dropped me off at school. I met Joey and Laura by my locker, which was just inside the back doors by the Orchestra Hall.

Joey said, "Are you ready?"

I said, "I can't."

He said, "What do you mean 'you can't'?"

I said, "I asked my mom and she said no."

Joey and Laura looked at each other. Laura said, "You asked your mom?"

I said, "What?"

Joey said, "Where is your mom?"

I said, "Illinois."

He said, "Exactly. Let's go. My car's out front."

I started following them. I didn't have the heart to tell them that my mom's antennae worked long-distance. *She'll never find out about it*, I told myself. *How can she? She's not even here.*

We drove out to the library at Indiana University East, the branch campus in Richmond, and took over one of their private rooms. The room was tight like a box and there were no windows—just a long desk and about a hundred chairs and lots of fluorescent lighting. We settled in and began to write, reading scenes aloud, sometimes writing on our own, sometimes arguing over this section or that section. Joey's writing was typically clever, Laura's madcap, mine heartfelt. We propped our feet on the table and leaned back in our chairs. We sprawled out on the table lengthwise. Laura and I sat on the floor under the table eating Oreos while Joey sat at the typewriter and took dictation. At lunchtime, we ordered our favorite food—Noble Roman's breadsticks with extra jalapeño cheese dip. Joey went outside to pay and intercept the delivery guy, and then smuggled the food inside in his backpack.

I called my dad at some point and told him that Joey would be driving me home, and then we stayed even later than school hours because we were light-headed by that time from no windows and too much artificial light and too many breadsticks and too much caffeine and too much writing. We came up with the silliest ideas and laughed over nothing.

That weekend, I practiced my mom's signature on a piece of her Carl Sandburg Oral History Project stationery because I would need a note. Joey would just make up one of his usual outpatient surgery excuses: *To Whom It May Concern, Joe Kraemer was absent Friday due to an appointment with Dr. Burge for Outpatient surgery. Thank you, E. M. Kraemer.* He was practiced in evil. Laura was experienced, too. She shrugged off danger. I, meanwhile, was a nervous wreck.

We went to the attendance office before school on Monday—each in a different line so as to avoid suspicion—and I held my breath as the lady behind the counter took my note. She looked it over, looked at me, and then smiled. She said, "I hope you're feeling better." And then I was free to go.

My mom came home days later and asked me how school was on Friday. "Good," I said, hoping my voice didn't sound too thin, a dead giveaway.

She looked at me calmly. "You didn't go, did you?" she said.

"What?"

"I know you didn't go to school," she said.

This was one of those superpowers mothers have like X-ray vision into your heart, or being able to humiliate you in public by not touching you or speaking, or knowing just what to say to make the tears go away.

I started to deny it, but then I just sighed and said, "I didn't go."

She said, "But we talked about this." I could tell she was

disappointed in me, which was always the very worst thing.

I said, "I know. And I'm sorry. But I wouldn't trade that day for anything."

There was a French exchange student living with the Lonigros named Sophie Gourdon. She was little and sturdy and had hair like a boy and barely spoke any English. She worshipped Joey. One afternoon Joey, Laura, and I posed for pictures in Laura's upstairs hallway, against the background of a white sheet covering the mirror that lined the wall facing the stairs.

Sophie took shot after shot of the three of us in our most glamorous poses. Jars of Vaseline and crazy hats, Coke bottles, shoes, a red rose, even a mannequin hand were introduced. Clothes were changed, exchanged, and then torn off. We posed for mug shots. We knew by this point that we might never finish *Judy on Purpose*. Our little one-act play was growing longer and longer. Laura's home life was becoming lonelier and harder to bear. She was taking care of herself and Monica, having to be big sister and parent. She threw herself into the play because, she said, she didn't think she would survive without it and us. Joey was struggling with issues he couldn't yet understand or voice. There was pressure from his parents, from the Catholic church he attended every Sunday—everywhere he looked he got the message loud and clear: *Be straight*. Only my home life seemed normal, except that my dad was busy all the time, missing dinners with my mom and me, not making it to school events, staying home during vacations while my mom and I went to North Carolina and New York, becoming more and more absent and distant in a way he hadn't been before.

Joey, Laura, and I were pulled in different directions,

though we still wrote and wrote. It wasn't about Tom Deh-ner anymore. It hadn't been for a long time. Our one-act play grew past one hundred pages, and overflowed into two hundred. We couldn't seem to stop ourselves.

Joey was working on the yearbook—editing it single-handedly because it had been dropped from the curriculum and he alone was willing to put in the hours needed to save it. So he had access to senior pictures. He blew up a shiny 8x10 of each cast member. The three of us drove to Dayton in Laura's silver Chevette—the one with the holes in the floor and no windshield wipers, Laura driving only in second gear because she'd never learned to drive a stick correctly—and climbed the steps of the Art Institute. We sat up at the top so we could look out over the city, and then we carefully arranged our cast in order of appearance before they blew away in the wind and we had to run chasing after them.

One day after school—sometime after the deadline had passed for Mr. Sizemore, when we now knew we would never see our play performed at Richmond High School—Joey and I sneaked into McGuire Hall. He moved about the stage, from place to place, while I watched him. "Rock will stand here," he said, "and Mother here. Lolita will be up there on the staircase they build—big and white and spiral-ing. A grand staircase, grander than the one they built for *Annie*. And Sharon over there. Father Douglas will enter there through the doorway, and here, center stage, is where Michael and Judy will stand." I took my spot. Joey moved into shadow. "Action," he said.

I turned to face the imaginary audience. If I squinted, I could just picture everyone—parents, teachers, faculty, and all of our classmates, gathered to watch the play we had worked so hard on.

"Here I am, plain old Judy Diamond from a little nowhere town you've never even heard of. A sister who's crazy, a suicidal brother, and a mother who doesn't understand me. Silly me, I thought things would change when I turned into the 'new Judy.' The 'new Judy.' Funny, I feel an awful lot like the old one."

I looked out over the imaginary heads of my classmates, my teachers, of everyone I knew. "If only Daddy hadn't gone away. Sometimes I wonder what everything would be like if he were still here. I don't think they realize just how much I miss him. And they don't understand. It would help if I could tell someone. If I had someone to talk to. But guess what? There's no one. There's only me." Sitting side by side, down in the front row, I could just see my parents—my mom *and* my dad—holding hands, happy.

I bowed my head. Then, from somewhere offstage—distant, but still quite audible—there was the sound of Joey singing: "God save our gracious Queen, Long live our noble Queen, God save the Queen: Send her victorious, Happy and glorious, Long to reign over us: God save the Queen!"

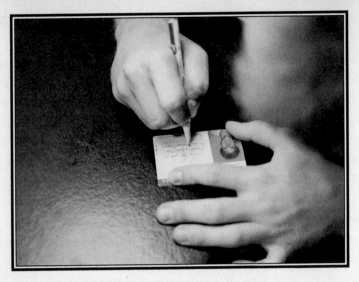

The simple art of making a fake ID

The Business of Drinking

After games we could be found doing what students through the years have done—cruisin' East Main, scarfin' on Big Macs at McDonald's, doggin' on some pizza at Noble Roman's, or gathering at someone's house for a party, always a welcome word at RHS. Then there were a few too easily entertained with their good friend "Mary Jane."

—1985 Pierian

When Tommy Wissel was a senior in high school, he was hired at the County Market, which was a big grocery store on the west side of town. He was supposed to report to work his first day at seven p.m., but for some reason he thought he was supposed to be there at five. When he showed up and they told him he was early, he walked over to

Hook's Drugs next door and stole a fifth of Scotch. He went back behind Hook's and County Market and played hackey sack and drank the entire bottle. Just before seven, he went back to work.

When he got there, he was taken on a tour of the market and shown what to do and given his badge and his apron. Then he was let loose on his own. He walked back to the liquor department and got a case of beer and they found him an hour later, surrounded by cans, having drunk his way through it.

He was brought into the back office. "We're calling your parents," his boss told him.

"No way," he said. He wasn't sticking around for that. He took off his apron and walked right out the front door. They called his dad anyway.

Tommy had been out with a girl from County Market a few times. She was pretty and fun and a good sport. Her name was Pam. She covered for him when his dad came to pick him up and he wasn't there. Tommy never went back to County Market, but he kept going out with Pam. As he said, "I knew she either loved me or pitied me and that any girl who would lie for me was a keeper."

For a long time, the drinking age in nearby Ohio was eighteen, but this changed minutes before the class of 1986 turned eighteen, which, of course, was horribly unfair. Luckily, if you lived in Richmond and went to Richmond High School, there were several options open to you for drinking, no matter your age. These options were:

The Grandfather Clause. In the 1980s, when the drinking age was raised from eighteen to nineteen and then to twenty-one, those of us (there weren't any in our class) who were eighteen before the drinking age changed were still allowed to buy alcohol and get served in bars. This meant driving over the state line to Ohio, where the drinking age had been eighteen, and then nineteen (the Grandfather Clause wasn't honored in Indiana because the drinking age had never been anything but twenty-one there).

The Lampost. This was a little restaurant-bar in New Paris, Ohio, about six miles from Richmond through the dark, open countryside and cornfields. The Lampost had been there since 1945, started by a man named Joe DiFederico, known to regulars as Uncle Joe. It was a place famous for its special spaghetti sauce and 3.2 beer. Generations of eighteen-year-old Hoosiers slipped across the state line to eat dinner and drink that 3.2 beer, which was a little less potent than actual beer but was still beer just the same. It was easy to get served at the Lampost. If all else failed, you knew you could count on 3.2 beer.

Fake IDs. Because they couldn't always drive to New Paris, some of my classmates took matters into their own hands. The Indiana driver's license had a dot matrix print scheme. Someone discovered that a simple pencil eraser could remove the ink on the surface of the license without creating too much of an obvious background change. It was easy to change a "1968" birth date into a "1965" by using a pencil—and even easier to change a "1967" into a "1963"—making someone twenty-one.

Ned Mitchell was the master. For instance, he turned Tom Mangas's "67" into a "63" using a very sharp pencil and some hair spray as a way to disguise the pencil dots, and then, one by one, he helped the rest of the fellas with their IDs. It always worked and usually passed close scrutiny, even a light thumb rub by a skeptical liquor store cashier.

In a pinch, though, if the cops pulled them over, a simple lick of the thumb and a single hard rub returned the date to normal.

The Liquor Barn. This was a dumpy little liquor store on the west side of town that was famous for serving even the most outlandish and improbable fake IDs. Laura was the only one in our group who had a fake ID (which said she was twenty-five). Jennie Burton would pull up in the parking lot before parties, the car idling in case we needed to speed away quickly, and Laura would go inside to buy whatever anyone wanted. She never once got carded even when she bought several bottles at a time. She would get back into the car and pass the bottles around and then we were ready to go to a party. Because we felt like we should, because it was somehow not as cool to show up empty-handed, everyone in our group chose a signature drink—mine was vodka, even though I hated the taste, because that's what Demi Moore drank in *St. Elmo's Fire* and I wanted to be just like her.

Parties. In the beginning, Joey, Laura, Jennie, and the rest of us weren't always told where the parties were. There were nights during our sophomore and junior years when we had to hunt them down. Part of the fun was talking about them and getting excited about them, in driving around in Jennie's station wagon trying to find them. The parties weren't widely advertised in an effort to keep out police, parents, and the wrong people. Once we found them, if we found them, we were welcome, but we envied the tightness and assuredness of Teresa's group or Tom Mangas's group. The Teresas and Tom Dehners of the world—the Sherri Dillons, the Jeff Shirazis, the Ronnie Stiers—knew exactly where they fit in. They didn't have to drive around searching for parties because they always knew ahead of time where they were—

sometimes at their own houses. They knew who would be
there and they knew everyone would show and they knew it
would be a great success. Other nights, we searched in vain
and eventually went home frustrated, never having found
them, knowing that somewhere in Richmond our classmates
were together having a good time without us.

There were always parties where there was a keg and
some sort of canned beer, and maybe something harder—
Southern Comfort was usually around. People smoked pot
and I was aware of the boys who did drugs, some of them
my friends who "dabbled" in them now and then. But there
was somehow an innocence to it all. It wasn't unusual to
see parents at parties, staying carefully out of the way. More
often than not they encouraged us to spend the night so we
wouldn't drive after drinking.

By senior year, Joey, Laura, and I were invited to the parties. Joey got fully drunk for the first time in his life at Tom
Dehner's house the fall of senior year and was very proud
because of where it happened. The best parties were at
Tom's house and at Rip's, where Tommy Wissel was always
yelling at me from an upstairs window or the roof or the TV
tower, or at Eric Ruger's, way out in the country under the
stars, or at Ian Barnes's, in a house with so many levels and
a pond. There was one girl who came to every single party
and always drank till she threw up—she threw up in bushes,
in bathrooms, in the backseats of cars. She was famous for it.
There were random party places like Devon Johnson's and
Cathy Brawley's and Jennie Burton's and Fiona Ferguson's
and Jeff Shirazi's, where there was an actual bonfire and a
hayride.

Laura and Monica gave a party at their house one night
when their dad was away. Angie Oler and Leigh Torbeck

danced on the fragile and expensive glass coffee table in the living room and broke it in half. Ross sat on an end chair and then Dwayne Flood sat on him and Cliff Lester sat on him until finally the chair collapsed. At the end of the night, the furniture was destroyed. Joey and Laura and Monica and I cleaned the house, and the next morning Laura and Monica Krazy Glued all the furniture before their dad got home.

Aldo Lonigro came in the door minutes after they were done gluing the broken chair and marched over to it. He said, "How are my girls? What did you do while I was gone?" He was in a chatting sort of mood. Laura and Monica stopped breathing as their dad sat down in the newly mended chair and kept talking. He was a large man—as big as a Vigran. They waited for it to collapse under his weight. He sat there, wanting to talk for a long time. By some miracle, the chair held firm.

Sometimes the parties weren't in a house, but on bridges, which weren't even bridges but really the sides of roads. It was always hard to find them, and we would drive and drive down country back roads, where everything looked the same, until we suddenly came upon a line of cars and a crowd of people. All the car radios would be tuned to the same channel—the music filling the night along with laughter and talking and the clattering of cans and bottles.

Commencement

And so we come to the end of yet another school year—our last year at RHS. As graduation approaches, we wonder how we could ever have been sophomores, why we ever felt the need to pray our way through Geometry and Chemistry. For many, the years have flown by. For others, these years have been an eternity. Each school year finds at RHS a class of students matured, educated, and longing to spread their wings; the spring of each year finds those wings stronger and itching to fly, and their masters ready to take to the air and see what the world offers to those who are brave enough to rise and embrace it, forever soaring, forever ascending, forever free.

One of Jennifer's many senior
picture poses

The Rules of Senior Poker

I just want the best wallet ever, is that too much to ask?

—*Jennifer to Joey, November 13, 1985*

Senior pictures were a Very Big Deal at Richmond High School. When we got them back from the photographer (there were three in town) in the fall of senior year, everyone walked the halls with a clear wallet-sized box that contained their favorite poses, and then the race was on to collect the best people. Joey, Laura, Hether, Jennie, Hill, and I were in a frenzy trying to accumulate them.

After our wallets were completed, there was nothing much to do but flip through them every now and then. We forgot about the pictures we had worked so hard to collect until one New Year's Eve at Hether's house, when Joey and Jennie came up with Senior Poker. We all sat in a circle and drank champagne as they explained the rules, which weren't really rules at all.

1. The rules had nothing to do with regular poker.
2. Everyone (Joey, Hether, Jennie, Hill, Laura, me) contributed the pictures from his or her wallet to the card pile.
3. Senior Poker could be played anywhere. We played one memorable game on a trip to Indianapolis, with Hether at the wheel of her Cougar, going a hundred miles an hour, me in the front seat next to her, and Joey, Jennie, and Hill in the backseat. I had to play Hether's hand for her. (Hether yelling: "Don't trade my Danny Allen! I know Joey wants it!")
4. The entire game was based on the Richmond High School social system. For instance: "I'll give you two Danny Dickmans for one Jeff Shirazi." Or, "I'll trade you a Cliff Lester and a Brian Lamar for a Ronnie Stier." Or, "My Ross Vigran or Robert Ignacio beats your Martha Schunks" (which were the equivalent of the nine of clubs or some other useless card).
5. It was a wild, fast-paced game. Pandemonium ensued and there were many disputes. You had to argue for points and negotiate the point value of people as you went. It was most challenging with the middle people on the social ladder—the Ian Barneses, the Deanna Hasketts—because you really had to argue their worth.
6. Tom Dehner trumped everyone, even Teresa Ripperger (who had points deducted for wearing a turquoise pantsuit in her pictures). But Rip trumped everyone but Dehner.

7. Tommy Wissel was the joker. We all screamed when we got him and he wasn't worth any points, even though everyone liked him. But I secretly didn't mind drawing his card. One, because it was my actual picture that he had given me with a flirty message on the back, and two, because he was so cute.

8. The game was over after all the cards had been traded. Whoever had the most points—that is, the pictures of the best people—won.

9. Once a round ended, everyone had to get their own pictures back, and you tried to steal someone else's pictures if they had someone you wanted. (Which was how Joey got pictures of Jeff Shirazi and Danny Allen, how Hether got Tom Dehner, how I got Teresa, and how Laura got Troy Hildreth.)

10. We never included our own pictures in the game.

Laura, Joey, and Jennifer finish out their Richmond sentence

Submissions

A student at Richmond Senior High School has before him the facilities with which to train himself for any profession of his choice, be it housekeeping, vocational work, engineering, or a job with the fine arts. The counseling department is always willing to help students with schedule problems, classroom problems, and after–high school plans.

— 1964 Pierian

Sometimes, instead of going to study hall, Joey and I went to the school library and sat in ascorner table at the back, where the ceiling seemed lowest and the lights were dimmest, and wrote stories together. Sheila Loeber walked in one day to return some books and we watched her as she stood at the desk. We wondered what she thought about and what it was like to be her—overweight, with a face covered in acne and oversized glasses, and body odor that everyone made fun of. She was a smart girl, a nice girl, but we felt sorry for her. She made us mad because she didn't do anything to help herself. When she left, we wrote a story about her hunting out hamburgers in the ceiling.

What we didn't say to each other, sitting in that library, was a lot. My dad was staying at the office more and more, which made me wonder if everything was okay. My mom and I ate dinner alone most nights, sometimes bringing out the blow-up plastic Christmas Santa and propping it in Dad's chair. "How was your day?" we would ask it, and then we would tell it all about ours. We called it Santa Dad. I didn't say anything about any of this to Joey.

Joey was struggling with feelings about himself, about boys, about girls, about expectations from his parents. There were inklings in his mind, but he didn't say anything about any of this to me. So we kept each other company and filled the silence with chatter and noise, with laughter and silly stories and loud songs, and everything else in the world but what was most on our minds.

We saw *St. Elmo's Fire* the summer before senior year on a night that seemed to be like any other. Pizza at Clara's. A quick drive-around looking for parties. When we could see that the town was dead, dead, dead, we drove out to the east side and over to the Mall Cinema, next to Mr. G's, which was, as usual, buzzing with people and loud music.

We had seen *The Breakfast Club*, of course, and liked it, although neither of us loved it the way everyone else seemed to. We liked stories about people older than we were because we liked people and things we could aspire to. Little did we know *St. Elmo's Fire* would become the most seminal movie we had ever seen and that it would change our lives. The scenery of Georgetown. Autumn in D.C. A close-knit group of friends that does everything together (and looks good doing it). Friends who understood each other and who always fit in with one another and their big-city school. Demi Moore's cool glasses and clothes and raspy voice. Her vodka. Her Jeep. Ally Sheedy's pearls. Judd Nelson's confidence. Andrew McCarthy's wit and coffin. All their crazy times, good and bad. The school itself. Rob Lowe. It was love at first sight.

That was the night we decided where we would go to college. It would be Georgetown. We would go there together and continue our great adventure, best friends forever. Jennifer and Joey. Joey and Jennifer. We had made up our minds.

"Don't you think you should apply to other schools?" my mom said.

"No. I'm going to Georgetown." I was in my room, sitting at my sewing desk, working on my college essay. My mom was standing over me, frowning.

"I understand that, but it's a very competitive school, and while I'm sure you'll be accepted, I think it's a good idea to apply to some other schools just to have a backup."

I sighed a little and laid down my pencil. She was, no doubt, thinking of my bad math grades (which, given my gene pool, couldn't be considered entirely my fault) and my low math SAT scores.

"Besides," she said, "I thought you wanted to go to New York and be an actress and a writer. Georgetown seems like a detour from that."

"Not really," I said. Honestly, I wasn't sure if George-town even offered a theater program or writing classes. Did they even have an English department? I was applying to the College of Arts and Sciences. Joey was applying to the School of Foreign Service. I pictured college parties with me in my Demi Moore glasses, swilling vodka, and making out with guys who looked just like Rob Lowe.

"What about UCLA? You mentioned that before."

"Too far for now." As much as I wanted to go far, far away from Richmond, and as much as I loved Los Angeles, I didn't want to go to the other side of the country. "Maybe for graduate school. I guess I could apply to somewhere in New York."

She said, "That sounds great. We can make a list." My mom loved to make lists. She made lists of everything—chores, groceries, things to do, lists for her work, lists for my dad, lists for me.

I said, "Oh good," but she missed the sarcasm.

In all, I applied to twelve schools because once I got started looking at brochures, I couldn't stop myself. Amherst, Princeton, Yale, Wake Forest, Davidson, William & Mary, a couple of New York schools, and a little liberal arts college just outside of New York City called Drew University, which my father told me about. My parents asked me to design my perfect college, apart from Georgetown, and I told them all the traits I was looking for: not too large, in or near a big city, a good liberal arts program. My dad had done some business at Drew (all these years later, I am still unclear what it was he did at Earlham), and he said he thought it fit my criteria.

One good thing about considering so many colleges was that I went to visit some—like the University of North Carolina–Chapel Hill (which threw fun parties but was way too big) and tiny Davidson just outside of Charlotte, North Carolina (which was way too small and isolated, even though the boys were good-looking).

For my essays, I wrote from the heart. *This is your opportunity to tell us about yourself,* the instructions said. *What would you most like the Admissions Committee to know about you when reading your application?*

Ever since we'd arrived in Richmond in my fourth-grade year, I had dreamed of the day I could leave. Now that moment was almost here. For the first time, I could practically see it.

I wrote: *In a town and place in which I have never felt quite at home, extracurricular activities and good friends have become very important to me. I seem always to need something which I can throw myself into wholeheartedly, and which will keep my spirits high during difficult times with school, peers, or other such problems . . .*

My career adviser was Linda McRally, who was pleasant and attractive. She had been a counselor at the high school for fifteen years, working in a cubicle in the Advisement Center at the end of the long upstairs hallway, which was always hot and stuffy, no matter what season we were in. She was Joey's adviser, too.

We each visited her to talk about college and our lives beyond RHS. Of course, Joey and I were both planning to go to Georgetown. But as Joey sat beside her desk in a hard plastic chair, he saw an advertisement behind her head for Hillsdale College in Michigan. He liked the look of the advertisement—an embossed gold "H" on navy blue, and underneath it just one word, "Leadership."

"Where do you plan to go to school?" Linda McRally asked Joey.

He said, "Georgetown."

She said, "Where else have you applied?"

He said, "The University of Chicago. I'll probably apply to Hillsdale, too." He decided it on the spot.

She said, "Where else?"

He said, "That's all. I want to get as far away from here as possible."

"And what do you plan to study?"

"I'm going to be a Kremlinologist." When she just stared at him, he said, "A Kremlinologist. An expert on the U.S.S.R. Either that or a lawyer. Or a playwright. Or a short story writer. In the big city."

She sat back and started flipping through his file and read some things. She closed it and folded her hands and smiled at Joey, but the smile was tired, especially around the eyes. She said, "There are so many good schools in Indiana. You shouldn't look down your nose at them just because they aren't in some big city. I think you should consider applying somewhere closer to home."

I sat in that same hard chair and had the same conversation with Mrs. McRally a few days later. She said, "Where do you plan to go to school?"

I said, "Georgetown." And I also listed the eleven other schools I was applying to just in case I wasn't accepted at Georgetown, even though I was sure I didn't need to apply to them since I couldn't imagine why Georgetown wouldn't be happy to have me.

She said, "And what made you choose these schools?"

It was such a strange question. I had chosen Georgetown

because of *St. Elmo's Fire*. The other schools I had chosen because they were in or near big cities.

When I didn't say anything she said, "What do you plan to do in college or after college?"

I said, "Oh, I plan to be a writer and an actress, but most likely a writer."

She sat there for a minute nodding. She said, "I think you should consider taking some secretarial classes in case the writing thing doesn't work out."

There were so many things I wanted to say like, *What kind of an adviser are you? Shouldn't you be telling me to dream as big as possible? Shouldn't you be encouraging students to dream big since so few of them do? I think more of them could stand to, if you ask me. Maybe if you'd encourage them they would. And then who knows where they'd go and what they'd do! And if the writing doesn't work out, who says I need to be a secretary? Why is that my one choice? Why not an astronaut? Or a rock star? Or a private detective? Or a plumber? Or president?*

But instead I smiled and stood up and walked out and never went back.

In February of our senior year, Joey and I drove to Dayton for an orientation about Georgetown University. By that time we had seen *St. Elmo's Fire* five hundred times and could recite entire passages. We traded lines back and forth as we drove and then we listened to the soundtrack, which, of course, we owned. We were quieter than usual on that trip because we were picturing ourselves in our new lives. There was a full moon, and I told Joey that Sue Weller had died.

For years he had worked at Morrisson-Reeves Library with her. She was the head of the Boys and Girls Department, the one who read us stories, back when we were children, in her soft, even voice. She was like a little girl herself, with long brown hair curled at the bottom, a pretty smile, a pretty face. She took her job seriously. She worked very hard. She had been married, but didn't have children of her own. I remembered her as a nice person, a quiet person who kept to herself.

She had taught Joey to read books on the Bookmobile. He was a little in love with her then and always chose which Bookmobile he wanted to work on during summers based on where she was working.

Somehow I had heard the news first. Sue Weller had driven home to Liberty the day before and shut the garage door and left the car running.

Joey said, "I can't believe she's gone."

"I'm sorry," I said. "It's so sad."

The music was still playing—the same music we always listened to—but everything felt different.

Joey said, "I wonder why she did it."

I said, "I don't know."

My seventh-grade English teacher had committed suicide. She'd gone home one night and driven into the garage and left the car running and her husband had found her. Afterward, all my classmates talked about how much they loved her and missed her. Everybody felt as if it was their fault that she killed herself. Maybe if they hadn't talked in class, or if they'd made a better grade on the spelling test. I was the only one who remembered how unpleasant she had been, how mean she could be, how unhappy she had seemed. Sue Weller wasn't any of these things, as far as we could see.

Joey said, "I wonder if there were things she wanted to do that she knew she'd never get to do."

I said, "Like dance with the New York City Ballet? Or be an archaeologist or a race car driver?"

"Or travel to Paris or see the pyramids."

We drove, looking out the windows at the darkness all around. There was never anything so dark as the highway in Indiana or Ohio, surrounded by cornfields at night. It is nothing but blackness everywhere and the empty road ahead.

Joey said, "I don't ever want to grow old or sad or lonely."

"We won't," I said. "We'll be young forever."

Orientation was at a hotel in downtown Dayton and for once we didn't get lost and nothing happened to the car. The room was packed. The only faces we recognized from Richmond were Beth Jennings and Mary Catherine Cox.

Beth was my friend and I liked her, but Joey was annoyed at seeing anyone we knew. "What are they doing here?" He was staring in particular at Mary.

I said, "Same as us I'm guessing."

He sighed. Beth waved us over. Joey said, "Well, don't think they're getting in."

We sat with them and wrote notes to each other and tried to be calm. We could feel the excitement in the air. Everyone seemed to feel it, not just us. But Joey and I knew that of all the people in that room, we were the ones who truly belonged there.

In March, we received our letters on the same day. *Dear Joe Kraemer, Dear Jennifer McJunkin*, they said. *The Committee on Admissions has completed its final review of applicants to the Class of '90 at Georgetown University. Following a careful consideration of all candidates, they have decided it will not be possible to offer you a place in the freshman class this year. Please accept our appreciation for the interest you have shown in Georgetown. We wish you every success in planning your further education.*

The next day Joey received an acceptance letter from Hillsdale College along with a full scholarship, and I received one from Drew University. We hadn't applied to any other schools together because it never occurred to us that we wouldn't actually get into Georgetown. We were shocked that we weren't accepted. We had been picturing ourselves there for so long that we couldn't imagine ourselves any other place. I would be Demi Moore. He would be Andrew McCarthy. We would ride around in Jeeps under brilliant autumn leaves and have cool friends and drink vodka and hang out at St. Elmo's Bar and always, always be together. Now just like that, the dream was gone.

That week, the Georgetown Hoyas lost to Michigan State, 80 to 68, in round two of the NCAA basketball tournament. For me, it was the last straw. The defeat was symbolic. They had lost. I had lost. I cried for an hour up in my green room watching the stupid game.

On Friday night, Joey and I packed up our Georgetown letters and a fifth of vodka he bought at the Liquor Barn and drove to Dayton. We climbed the steps of the Art Institute, long after closing, and sat huddled against the wind and the cold. The moon and the stars were almost too bright. There was something unfair about them. We unfolded our letters and read them out loud and then I tore mine into bits and watched them fly away into the air. We passed the bottle back and forth, back and forth until it was time to go home.

Jennifer, her parents, and their dog Jamey

Homework

First of all let me tell you about my family. My father Jack, my mother Penny, my cat Princess, my cat Michael, and my dog Jamey. Also myself, Jennifer.

—*Jennifer McJunkin, "My Life in Indiana," September 25, 1977*

When I was little, I used to play a game. I would try to decide who I would live with if my parents split up. It was a game I took very seriously, largely because I knew it would never happen. I would lie in bed or in my green beanbag and really think about it.

I knew I would probably choose my mom because she and I were so alike. We both laughed and had fun. She was bright and bubbly. Every night before I went to bed, she told me she loved me. She told me again in the morning. She said she wanted it to be the first thing I heard when I woke up and the last thing I heard before I went to sleep. Everyone loved her, most of all me. My dad was quieter, more intense, more brooding. He worked all the time and got impatient because many things got on his nerves.

But he and I were alike, too. I had his brown hair and brown-green eyes that looked more brown than green but were really more green than brown. I had his stubbornness and his short temper. He was also more relaxed than my mom about some things—he got my mom to loosen up and not watch me so closely and let me be. He was less perfect than my mom, more openly and obviously flawed, and I knew I was that way, too. No one was as perfect as my mom.

Mom was also a writer, and this was something I was thinking about being. Writing was certainly something I liked doing, ever since I was a little girl and she had instilled writing time into my daily routine. My mother was the director of the Carl Sandburg Oral History Project. She had organized his papers at his North Carolina home, Connemara, and traveled the country interviewing people who knew Sandburg—Gene Kelly and Steve Allen, whom we met in Los Angeles; musician Pete Seeger, who stayed at our house in Hidden Valley; journalist Harry Golden; and even a man in Chicago who had just gotten out of prison for murdering his wife. My dad hovered around during that interview in case my mom needed protection, and I hovered around just in case I could hear something about his time in prison. She made speeches at universities and historical societies and now she was writing a book on Sandburg—the first comprehensive biography of him ever written. Sandburg's own agent, Lucy Kroll, was representing her. My mother's work was horribly exciting.

I loved my dad. When I was little, we were the best of friends. We were more playmates than father-daughter. We got into mischief together and pulled silly pranks on each other and got into trouble with my mom. But as I grew older, we suddenly had very little to talk about. He didn't want to hear about boys and he didn't like my music. My mom would say, "Give it a chance, Jack." And he would say, "That isn't music. How can you listen to it with her?" And Mom would say, "Because Jennifer is interested in it and I'm interested in Jennifer."

My dad was an only child, too, and we were sometimes competitive. When I was little, my mom had to talk to him about letting me win at Uncle Wiggly and Chutes & Ladders. "For God's sake, Jack," she would say. "She is a five-year-old girl." But this didn't matter to him. Whatever game we played, my dad wanted to win, and I was the same exact way. Whoever lost would fall into a deep, dark sulk, so silent and forbidding that no one could speak to us for hours after the game was over.

Worse than this, my father ate all the good things that came into the house, hoarding them like a squirrel gathering food for the winter. Whenever there was anything delicious to eat—cookies or lemon bars or cheese biscuits or cupcakes from Joy Ann Bakery—my mom had to dole out fair and equal shares of them (drawing a line down the pan of lemon bars and carving "J" for Jennifer on one side, and "D" for Dad on the other) and then hide the rest somewhere in the kitchen so that my dad wouldn't eat them all. He always, always found them, though, and ate well into my share and my mother's. I would climb up onto the kitchen counter and reach into the very back of the cabinet and pull out the white bakery box, and there would be only three cookies where before there had been eight. In times like these, my mom would give me her share and what, if anything, was left of mine. She almost never got a delicious thing to eat herself.

And my dad was busy. He was the busiest man I knew. In addition to working at Earlham as the business manager and as the director of planned giving (jobs he did simultaneously and which I never understood no matter how many times he explained them to me), he taught Asian history and religion and a squash course at the gym. He chaired the faculty nominating committee, the first administrator to be elected by the faculty to that position, among other committees. He served on the boards of the local mental health center and the Richmond Symphony Orchestra, ran at least five miles daily, if not more—twenty-six on weekends. And to top it all off, he was always cooking. He was widely acclaimed in East Central Indiana for his culinary skill. (My parents had even written a cookbook together— *The I Hate to Chew Cookbook: A Gourmet Guide for Adults Who Wear Braces*, inspired by my mom getting braces at age forty. Then my parents and I wrote *Teen Cuisine: A Cookbook for Young People Who Wear Braces*.) My dad could whip up shrimp bisque or Marchand di Vin for sixty people easily, and was always trying to teach me the right wine to go with beef Wellington. This was maddening because when you are a teenager, all you want to eat are normal things like hamburgers and Kraft Macaroni & Cheese out of the box. My father made his macaroni and cheese from scratch. It took hours. He even made the noodles by hand.

Time and again, I decided that I would definitely live with my mother.

• • •

One day, toward the end of my senior year, I was standing on my head, trying to reach the Men at Work album that had fallen behind my bookcase. There was a knock at the door.

"Come in!" I yelled.

There was a pause, and then the door opened and my father walked in. I immediately tried to think of what I might have done wrong because he never came to my room. He didn't like the clutter—the clothes everywhere and the glasses that needed washing. He didn't like the posters of boys and rock stars that hung on my walls, and he didn't like the music I was always playing on the stereo he had built for me himself out of the finest hi-fi components.

"Jenge?" It was his private nickname for me, based on the name I called myself when I was little, in the days before I could pronounce Jennifer.

"Yes?"

"I need to talk to you," he said.

"Okay." I sat down on my bed and he sat next to me.

We sat there a long time in silence until finally he said, "I don't want you to think that there's anyone else. It's important that you know that. But your mother and I are separating, and she wanted me to tell you because it's not her idea, it's my idea. I just can't. I just can't have a family right now. It isn't you and it isn't her. It's me."

Your mother and I are separating.

I felt as if I had been slammed in the head with something, like the time my junior high school gym teacher made me guard Jody Starn in basketball, all three hundred pounds of her, and she had sent me flying into the gym wall. I tried not to cry because my dad hated tears more than he hated my music and my boy talk. I thought about Alex Delaney's parents who never got along and how I had felt so sorry for him. I thought about Laura's parents—her mom in Dayton, her dad always gone. I sat there thinking about how your entire life could change in an instant.

"We are going to stay together for the rest of your senior year. We don't want you to have that disruption. We'll stay here together in this house, and after you graduate, we'll separate. But you cannot tell anyone, not even Joey. We don't want this getting out into the community. We have to entertain together for my work. We don't want people talking."

I didn't say anything or ask anything. I just sat there, staring at the yellow of my bedspread, thinking how bright it was, wondering why I'd never asked to paint my green walls when I didn't even like green, I liked purple.

"I'm so sorry," he said. "I'm so sorry."

And I realized I was crying, and, worse, he was crying, which was something I had never seen my dad do except when our Scottish terrier, Jamey, died, and that I had expected because he loved Jamey, probably even more than he loved my mom and me.

He hugged me then, and it wasn't awkward. It was wonderful. I couldn't remember the last time he'd hugged me. I used to ride around on his shoulders as a little girl and pat him on his bald head. I used to hold on to his arms—tanned with golden hairs that turned copper in the sun—when I was learning to skate.

He pulled away and then my mother came in and she was crying, too. My dad left and my mom sat down and she and I just cried and cried. But even then, I didn't believe it. *This is not happening,* I kept thinking, *this is not real. This can't happen, not to us.*

The next day, everything was like normal. My dad got up and I got up and my mom had been up for hours. The three of us sat at the breakfast table not talking because my dad and I were not morning people and didn't like to talk before eleven a.m. My mom hummed to herself and tried to subdue her morning energy.

Later, my mom told me we could talk if I wanted to, that it was important to talk and get things out. "You have to let the tears come," she always said. "Because if you don't, they will come out eventually—in depression, in anger, yelling, slamming doors, throwing a hairbrush against the wall," which was something I had been known to do. But I told her I was fine.

I went up to my green room and called Joey.

"What are you doing?" he said.

"Nothing," I said.

"What's going on?" he said.

"Oh," I said. "Nothing much." It was the start of keeping things in, of holding them inside and not sharing them with the people closest to me. It stung then like a fresh slap, but it would become easier and easier with time.

He said, "Do you want to go to a movie? I think I can get the car." Sometimes Joey had to share the car with his brother Mitchell, and we couldn't always have it when we needed it.

I said, "Okay."

He said, "Or we can go to Dayton instead."

I thought of driving fast and Billy Idol and turning the music up loud, loud, loud, and I said, "That sounds better."

He said, "I'll be there soon." We hung up and I waited in my room, watching out the window for Joey, so I wouldn't have to sit downstairs and talk to my mom.

Matt Ashton, Jennifer McJunkin, Hillary Moretti, Jennie Burton, Joey Kraemer, Diane Armiger, Brian Yoder, Danny Allen, Ricky Grimes, and unidentified girl—where Laura Lonigro should be—at prom

Prom

My dress is beautiful! Wonderful! Gorgeous! It's white and light blue (striped) Gunne Sax. It's kind of a Scarlett O'Hara kick-ass dress. What does yours look like, Hill?

My dress is plain and pink and pitiful. (If the shoe fits . . .)

—Jennifer and Hillary, exchanging notes in Russian Literature

Our prom, the fifty-third Richmond High School prom, was held at an off-school site for the first time since the 1930s—in the Stardust Ballroom of the newly reno-vated Radisson Hotel (the old Leland Hotel, built on the

site of a casket factory) just off the Promenade downtown.
The theme was "Steppin' Out."

Joey decided I should go to prom with Ronnie Stier. This
was fine except that Ronnie and I both had other plans.
I wanted to go with Matt Ashton and Ronnie wanted to
ask Tricia Ahaus. Matt and I were writing each other letters faithfully and talking on the phone. We saw each other
on school breaks. The closer I got to graduation, the more
detached I became from Richmond and everything in it,
and that meant the boys there, too. Besides, Ronnie and
I were good friends—bonded over the history team—and
nothing more.

But Joey thought Ronnie was cute and deserved a try. So
he organized a Get Ronnie to Ask Jennifer to Prom Campaign. This consisted of Joey writing Ronnie notes every day
in AP History class, hinting about prom and me. When he
wasn't doing this, he worked on Cathy Brawley, Eric Ruger's
girlfriend, trying to get her to help him. Brawley thought all
girls were whores because they were threats to her relationship, especially girls who were friends with Eric, like I was.
So Joey made sure to tell her things like, "Jennifer was just
saying what a cute couple you and Ruger make and how she
hopes you get married one day," because he knew how much
Cathy would like hearing it. He also worked on Teresa, who
was good friends with Ronnie. And on me. At night, he
would talk about it on the phone to me, trying to convince
me to send Ronnie a note myself—something provocative
that would get his attention and make me stand out in his
mind.

"Good Lord," I said. I was writing a letter to Matt on my
best stationery in purple ink. One reason I liked Matt was
that he represented Somewhere Else. The last two months

of my senior year, I felt strange and distant. There was a separation from my friends that I couldn't bridge because of this thing with my parents I couldn't talk about. My parents were still living together, of course. We'd never said another word about their separation. Everything was exactly like it was before my dad came into my room and told me he couldn't have a family—we ate dinner together at night, went to movies and restaurants together, my parents smiled and talked and rarely argued. I started thinking I'd imagined the whole thing. With Matt, who wasn't there and who didn't live there, I felt more like myself. I didn't tell him what was happening at home, but I could still talk to him and feel somewhat normal.

"Just do it," Joey said. "Ronnie will look good in a tux. You'll look good together."

Maybe Joey was right. He was right, after all, about most things. Well, some things. Why not this? Besides, I missed Matt. It was hard being so far away from him. It might be nice to go with someone here in town. I put the letter to Matt aside. Sometimes it was exhausting thinking about my feelings all the time. "Okay," I said. "Fine. What should I say?"

The next day I sent Ronnie the following note in AP History class.

Me: *Does that offer still stand?*
Ronnie: For what?
Me: *Sharing your locker, remember?* [Note: He never offered to let me share his locker.)
Ronnie: Did I ever offer that? [Note: He didn't.] It must have been one of my weaker moments. You'd have to ask Todd. [Irwin.]

Me: *Oh. But would you mind? I mean, I won't*
               if you don't want me to, but I <u>hate</u> having to
               share that locker with all of those girls—I don't
               like any of them anyway.

Ronnie: We don't have much room, either. But it's
               all right with me. I'll ask Todd. And all this
               time I thought you loved all those girls in
               your locker. If I was you I would throw the
               extras out.

Me: *It's impossible—I think they breed in there or*
               something. I hate them all. And if I did move
               into your locker, I know you wouldn't regret
               it—I promise not to throw my personal things
               everywhere . . . [Note: A line Joey told me
               to say. Like by writing "personal things,"
               it would make Ronnie picture sexy bras or
               lingerie, neither of which I owned. The
               closest thing I had to a sexy bra was the
               underwear my grandmother Cleo gave me
               every year for my birthday, which, while
               lacy and skimpy, was always three sizes too
               small because, compared to her, she thought
               everyone was flat-chested.]

Ronnie: All right. I guess you'll have to use the bot-
               tom. But watch out for the rats that live on
               my history book.

Me: *Rats?!!! Well, I guess it can't be any worse than*
               Michelle Zimmerman or Sara Ansel or any of
               the other fifteen people in there.

And on and on . . . I never did move into his locker,
of course, but Joey kept up his campaign. Ronnie finally

told him, "I guess I'll have to talk to my adviser on personal affairs—Rip—to find out if I'm going or not."

And Joey was off to the racetrack to get to Rip first.

Never had so much thought and effort gone into prom planning. Meanwhile, Joey was dealing with his own little drama. Joey wanted to go to the dance with Diane Armiger, even though he was dating Jennie Burton. This was further complicated by the fact that our friend Hillary, who was Jennie's best friend, thought Joey was going to ask her because someone (probably Ross) had told her so.

So thanks to Joey I now thought I wanted to go to prom with Ronnie Stier. Joey wanted to go with Diane Armiger. Brian Yoder, my seventh-grade boyfriend, wanted to go with Laura, who wanted to go with him, too. Hillary wanted to go with Joey. Jennie wanted to go with Joey. Brian Yoder's best friend Ricky Grimes wanted to go with Laura.

Ronnie told Joey that, while I was good-looking and smart, I was maybe too smart and not as good-looking as I seemed to think I was. Besides, he and I were just good friends, bonded over the history team—the same thing I had told Joey at the start. Ronnie asked Tricia Ahaus, who was going with someone else, and he ended up instead with Paula Snow. I asked Matt Ashton, who I'd wanted to go with in the first place, even though he lived in South Carolina. I said to Joey, "Why did you even get me thinking about Ronnie? You knew I wanted to go with Matt!"

Joey said, "Because I thought we'd have fun with him."

Danny Allen asked Diane, which upset Joey, who then asked Jennie, which made Hillary furious. Ricky Grimes asked Laura first, so she went with him, which made Brian Yoder angry. Ricky and Brian were best friends, and Ricky suggested Brian take Hill, who didn't have a date. Hether asked Jay Something-or-Other, who didn't even go to RHS. She had met him at the Hardees drive-through.

The twelve of us had dinner beforehand at Jennie's house. Hillary didn't speak to anyone. Ricky didn't speak to Laura, who had made out with Brian before Ricky picked her up and before Brian picked up Hillary. Laura and Brian played footsie under the table. Hill went outside to smoke the joint she always carried in her purse. Jay sat on one side of me, staring at his plate, self-conscious over his bad grammar and terrified of all of us. Matt and Joey talked and laughed. Hill finally snapped and yelled something at Jennie, who told her to grow up. Diane asked us if she should wear the white scarf she brought with her, and we all told her yes, even though we thought it looked hideous. Danny picked at his powder blue tuxedo, which he said he only wore because he was late picking up his tux, and by the time he got there it was the only one left in his size.

There was a preparty at Eric Ruger's house, and we stopped by there briefly—even though it meant driving far out of our way, deep into the country. In our car, Matt and I were the only couple talking to each other and the only one who stayed together at the party. After an hour, we all came back into town in a caravan and went to the Radisson.

By the end of the evening, Laura had disappeared. Brian got high in the parking lot with some of his hood friends. Ricky sat in the lobby smoking cigarettes. Diane ran around looking for her white scarf, which had gone missing. Hether and Jay were making out in his truck. Jennie and Joey had lost each other, and Joey and I were dancing near Tom Dehner, spinning wildly about in place, while Matt watched.

"Come here," he said, trying to catch me. "Dance with me."

"I *am* dancing," I said. I wanted to say: *I'm dancing with Joey. I'm almost dancing with Tom Dehner!*

Afterward, there was a party upstairs in Todd Irwin's room. Almost the entire floor was rented out to people in our class. Laura had gotten us a room next door to Todd's. We fixed our hair and makeup—Aqua Net spraying everywhere—while the guys sat on the bed and watched TV and drank from bottles of Southern Comfort that Laura had bought earlier at the Liquor Barn, with her fake ID that said she was twenty-five, even though she was clearly wearing her prom dress.

"Are we sleeping here, too?" Matt said. He had to shout it over all the noise.

"No," I said. Some of my classmates were spending the night with their dates, but that was definitely not happening in my prom party. I looked at all the miserable faces in our room. "We're just here to have fun and fix our hair."

We went next door and joined everyone else. Rip and Tom Dehner were fighting again. Tommy Wissel jumped from bed to bed, knocking people off. Ross and Cliff Lester ran up and down the hallway, banging on doors. Everybody was smoking and drinking, and eventually my head started to spin from the fumes of the smoke and the alcohol.

Then, once again, we piled into our cars and drove deep into the country, under the stars and the too-bright moon, to Eric Ruger's farm for the real postparty. There was more running around and drinking and smoking and lots of Rush on the stereo and Phil Collins and other bands like Led Zeppelin and Yes and AC/DC. I lost track of Joey along the way, and most of our group was gone by that point. Matt and I drove home.

"Your friends are fun," he said. I wondered if he could possibly mean it based on the evening we'd just lived through.

"I'm glad you came," I said.

We tiptoed inside, but my mom was waiting up, as she always did. We told her about the dinner, the dance, the party, and then she said good night. We went downstairs to the family room and lay down on the floor. We kissed for a long time.

Matt pulled away and leaned on one elbow. I was lying flat on my back, shoes off, my pale blue and white Gunne Sax skirt and crinoline pillowing out around me. Matt looked dark and dashing, like Jeff Shirazi, only taller and leaner and, I thought, cooler. I loved his southern accent.

"Do you want to?" he said.

"I do," I said. And I did.

"Me too."

I was quiet. *Was this it?* Was this *the* right and magic moment I'd been waiting for with *the* right and magic boy? I thought about Zelda and Scott Fitzgerald and the extraordinariness of their love. *I don't want to live—I want to love first, and live incidentally,* Zelda wrote to Scott in 1919. I thought of all my classmates across town who were probably having sex for the first or second or twentieth time even as I was lying there trying to make up my mind.

I said, "But I don't think we should."

"No, I don't guess we should."

"It's stupid," I said, "because everyone is doing it. I'm sure everyone thinks I've been doing it. And I can't imagine doing it with anyone else right now. But I just don't think I'm ready. I feel like such a baby."

"That's fine," Matt said. "We can just stay right here and do this."

He kissed me again, sweetly. There was passion and warmth. It was pure and electric all at once. I thought of enormous Tim Bullen hoisting himself on me until I pushed him off and of going parking with Tom Mangas in his Party Car. I thought of making out with Troy Hildreth in Eric Ruger's barn and of kissing Sean Mayberry at the drive-in. I thought of Eric Lundquist and felt a pang, and thought of Alex and felt guilty.

"I love you," Matt said.

"I love you, too," I said back. I was glad Ronnie Stier had asked Paula Snow to prom instead of me.

Jennifer giving her graduation speech at commencement

Castles in the Air

Me: I'm so nervous—today I'm trying out for graduation
        speaker. Wish me luck!

Hether: Best of luck! But *when* you get it *don't* be BORING!

By early May 1986, most of us had stopped paying attention in class. There wasn't any need to. If we were going
to college, we'd already been accepted. Some of us weren't
going to college. We were getting jobs instead. Or going in
to the military. Or not even graduating. We only had a few
more weeks of school and you could just feel the buzz in the
air—*freedom*.

There were parties every weekend and we went to all
of them. On a Saturday, Tamela Vance threw one at her

grandfather's house. Joey and Jennie kissed on the porch swing while Rob Jarrett started a game of volleyball without nets in the dark. The party was eventually broken up by the police who wanted to see IDs. Long before that happened, Laura and I left in her little Chevette, driving around town by ourselves. She was upset about her parents and needed to talk. I couldn't tell her about my own parents, so I listened. But I knew just what she was going through. We were the two loneliest girls in Richmond.

A week or so later, Joey wrote me a note. He always hated to be left behind. He knew that what was happening with Laura and that whatever was happening with me that I wasn't talking about was something he couldn't participate in. He wrote: *I will always think of Tamela's house as a strange moment in our friendship—one of the only lonely moments. It's a peculiar time that leaves me feeling odd and strangely mistaken somehow, as if I had turned to look behind me on a street I thought I knew well, only to find I was not on the street I had thought I was on.*

At school, we were barely listening when announcements were made that tryouts would be held for graduation speaker. Unlike most schools, the valedictorian wouldn't automatically be giving the speech. If the valedictorian or salutatorian, or anyone else for that matter, had any desire to speak, they had to audition, and a panel of teachers would choose three speakers. This was a way to be fair to the entire student body and give everyone a chance. Tom Mangas, who had always been top of our class and who was, of course, our valedictorian, couldn't believe it. I was in U.S. Government with him when the announcement was made, and I thought he was going to have a seizure.

He said, "This is grossly unfair."

I said, "You'll do fine, Tom. You're a good speaker. Just write a great speech and prove to everyone why you're valedictorian in the first place." But I was secretly thinking how happy I was I'd had all those years of speech team training. *I'll give you a run for your money, Tom Mangas,* I thought. *You'd better write a damn good speech because I am going to kick your ass.*

On the day of auditions, a surprising number of students showed up in hunky Mr. Alexander's room, considering it was after school and a sunny day and an activity that wasn't required and, on top of it all, something that took some actual work and effort—meaning you had to have written a speech and done some preparation ahead of time. Tom Mangas was there, of course. And Joey. Most of the members of our former speech team—the real speech team, not the fake one that Joey and I had created—a handful of other students, some I didn't recognize, others you would expect from student congress . . . and me.

My speech was called "Castles in the Air," which was based on a quote by Henry David Thoreau that my mom had suggested—"If you have built castles in the air, your work need not be lost; that is where they should be. Now put the foundations under them." It was all about building your dreams as big as possible.

This was something I'd always believed in and something I'd always tried to share with the people around me, even if they didn't want me to. In seventh grade, a group of my friends came over to my house one afternoon to play. Before we went outside, I made them write essays about their life's ambitions. When they were done, I graded them on their ability to dream big. "You girls can do better than this," I told them. "You're selling yourselves short. I want you to open your minds and let those dreams in, and even if you think they're impossible, you need to remember that no dream is too big." When I asked them to rewrite their essays, my friend Beth Jennings said she would rather play tennis in the street. "You have all your life for tennis," I said. "But we need to get these dreams right while we still can."

Mr. Alexander, tan in his dark suit, the man who should have been our speech coach, officiated at the auditions. We spoke in front of the judges while our classmates waited in the hallway outside. When I finished, they thanked me, Mr. Alexander smiled his white, white smile, and I walked out the door.

Tom Mangas stood there waiting. He was agitated. I couldn't ever remember seeing Tom agitated, Tom who was one of the coolest boys in school. He said, "How did it go?"

I said, "Oh, pretty well."

"Pretty well?"

"They seemed to like it."

"Why? Did they say anything?"

"No. But I've done so many speech meets, you know," casually emphasizing my speaking experience, "you learn to read the judges. Good luck with yours, Tom."

"Thanks."

The following Monday, the results were in. The three students chosen to speak at the one hundred fifteenth commencement of Richmond High School were Stephanie Felix, Debbie Pierson, and Jennifer Niven McJunkin. Beth Jennings and Joe Kraemer would give the invocation and benediction during the Honors and Awards Assembly.

I saw Tom Mangas in the hallway after first period. He was furious.

• • •

I turned eighteen on May 14. To celebrate, my parents hosted a special birthday dinner with Jennie, Hill, Diane, Hether, Laura, and Joey. When it was present-time, my friends wrapped the remote control from our downstairs TV in a brown paper bag and told me to open it. It was very funny, but then I said, "Um, where's my real present, guys?" And that's when they gave me the Swatch they'd all chipped in for.

Then they gave me lots of cards, and Diane had picked out one with six Budweisers on it, and Hether's face turned very red because she was laughing so hard and could barely breathe. My dad ran in and out of the kitchen serving food, which he loved doing. This was when he was happiest. My mom made sure everyone had enough to drink and eat. They bumped into each other and laughed. My friends didn't notice but I told myself, *If you don't talk about the separation and your parents don't talk about the separation, maybe it's not really happening. Maybe they're not really going to break up. Maybe they're working everything out. Maybe everything will be just fine.* Everything looked just fine to me.

The day before, I'd received a package from Matt Ashton: a romantic-type card with lots of lovely writing in it (which I'd already committed to memory) and a cute stuffed dog, which I was still carrying around. During the party, I kept it on my lap and every now and then I picked it up and squeezed it.

On graduation day, my dad's parents—Granddaddy Jack and Grandmama Cleo—came from Asheville. Grandmama's eyes were damp as soon as she got there. She kept dabbing at them so I wouldn't notice.

The girls wore white, the boys wore red. The weekend

before, my mom and I had shopped for the perfect gradua-tion dress. I found just the thing I was looking for at Zelda's Vintage Clothing on the Promenade, a little cubbyhole above the Whitewater Opera House. I was mad about Zelda Fitzgerald and couldn't believe the name on the door when I walked past it. You had to walk up a narrow flight of dark, dark stairs, and there at the top was this tiny little room with just two racks of clothes, a million hats pinned to the walls, some old shoes heaped about on the floor, and an old glass counter full of earbobs (as my grandmama Eleanor called them) and other jewelry. I knew the dress when I saw it. It was red and white polka dots like the RHS school colors, and had a twirly skirt, but was snug in a good way every-where else. It fit perfectly.

Because I was one of the speakers, I sat on stage in the Tiernan Center with Stephanie and Debbie. Tom Mangas, as our president and valedictorian, sat up there also. The crowd was rowdy and restless—this was the gym, after all. There were at least five thousand people there, sitting up in the bleachers, and they stomped and cheered at every opportunity. They talked to themselves and acted like they were at a basketball game, not just during the Processional— "Pomp and Circumstance," of course—but when Principal Brist was giving his welcome and introductions and when local youth minister Lee Gulley was giving the invocation.

When it was time for my speech, my mother, sitting in the audience with my grandparents and my father, was prepared to stand up and silence anyone who talked or cheered or didn't pay attention. As I walked to the podium, I thought about something Tommy Wissel had reminded me of—a time in ninth grade, when he was still new to Den-nis Junior High School from the Catholic school, and we were in science class together. Mr. Stoner assigned everyone oral reports, and one by one we all got up to give them. No one paid attention to anyone else—it was like an unspoken agreement: "I won't pay attention to you when you're up there and you don't pay attention to me." Everyone was sleeping and passing notes and talking, doing their hair, looking at their shoes.

I'd actually worked hard on my report, so when I walked up to the front of the room and no one paid attention, I stood up there and looked at everyone and said, "I'm not standing up here to give this report to myself. I'm not doing it just for fun or to hear myself talk, people. So pay attention or I'm sitting down!" Tommy dropped everything and so did everyone else and no one said a word during my speech. "It freaked us out," Tommy said. "I thought, 'Man, this girl actually put some work into this. That's the kind of student I should be.'" He went home that night and read the chapter I'd covered in my report just to see if I'd gotten everything right. Years later, he could still recite entire lines from my speech.

Now on stage in the Tiernan Center, I said into the microphone: "All of us here tonight have our own castles in the air. We dream of what the future holds for us. I remember how frightened I was on the first day of high school. Coming to this huge place after junior high was like starting over. Now as we leave high school, we are starting over one more time. Thoreau said, 'If you move confidently in the direction of your dreams, you can live the life you imagine.'"

There was applause afterward, but the most amazing thing had happened while I was talking: everyone seemed to be listening. And they listened to Stephanie after me. And after her, to Debbie.

We accepted our diplomas from board president Jack T. Miller. He told us: "Life is like a journey up a mountain. I congratulate you on reaching this plateau. But the plateau is very narrow. Don't fall off. Now that you have reached this plateau, continue your education and prepare for the rest of your lives."

Each time someone walked across the stage, the audience shouted and cheered and wolf whistled. Every now and then someone would yell, "It's about time!" Or, depending on how long the person graduating had been at RHS, "It's about fucking time!" When I stood up to get my diploma and shake Mr. Miller's hand, I thought, *This is it. You're done with this place. You can finally get out of here and move onward, upward, out of Richmond like you've always wanted to.* It felt like everything was starting but ending all at once. For a moment I wanted to hand back the diploma and sit down in my seat and go back to class on Monday and stop everything, freeze it just as it was. I didn't know what would happen next—to me, to my parents, to my friends, to my family, to . . . everything. And I suddenly wanted all of it to stay the same.

When the last person walked across the stage to get her diploma, the audience stood up—a few at a time at first and then everyone together—and clapped and shouted. It was a sea of red and white. Principal Kenneth Brist presented our class to acting superintendent Timothy Jackson and then we jumped out of our seats, pumping fists, throwing diplomas and hats into the air, hugging.

Diane Armiger and Jennifer McJunkin—with vodka—at Jennie Burton's graduation party

Graduation Party

Knowing only that we were young,
And drunk,
And twenty,
And that the power of mighty poetry
Was within us,
And the glory of the great earth
Lay before us . . .

> —*Thomas Wolfe*

The party was at Jennie's. Because we were in the inner circle, Joey, Hether, Hillary, Laura, Diane, and I were invited to stay the night. We were up and down the house, in and out of all the bedrooms, in places that were off-limits to everyone else. The general public had to stay outside—in the driveway or in the barnlike structure that sat up near the house and whose purpose we were never sure of. What could it possibly be for except to serve as a hangout for us? It had a loft with high beams and was decorated with signs we had stolen and things we had spray-painted, like "Stop, Drop, & Roll One" and "Let's Go All the Way" and "Red Devils Rule."

Mr. and Mrs. Burton were on hand to supervise, but they stayed in the house while we ran wild everywhere. They mostly made sure no one had too much to drink or got behind the wheel of a car.

Everyone was there, although it was a blur. We were suddenly free. We were no longer high school students. We were graduates now, in the real world. Teresa Ripperger and Tom Dehner showed up. He was wearing a red corduroy baseball cap and looked strong and sunburned, the best we'd ever seen him. At some point, not long afterward, Laura and Tom disappeared together. Joey and I couldn't believe it. Was it possible that one of us, after all this time, had gotten him? We held our breath, because it was almost like it was happening to us.

Allison Bing, who was still in high school, followed Joey around like a puppy. Ross had his hands full with both Tally Bland and Amy Johnson, two of his ex-girlfriends. Ted Fox was trying his pickup lines on anyone who would listen ("You're so fine, I'd like to make you a Fox!"). Diane and I danced madly in the barn, and then Sean Mayberry found me and we went off to the woods to make out. He gave me a hickey on my neck and I ran away from him laughing. Jeff Shirazi passed out in Jennie's barn, very early, and we all visited him to see how he was doing. Hether lay down after a while and took a nap beside him. Jennie came to find us to say Hill was passed out in the upstairs bedroom because the pot was laced. We all stood over her—Joey, Diane, Jennie, and me (Laura was still nowhere to be found)—and tried to decide if we should get Jennie's mom. Then we heard shouting, and, back outside, Laura went running by wearing Tom Dehner's baseball cap, and Teresa stalked past, on the hunt for either Tom or Laura, whichever one she could find. Then there was more dancing, more drinking—Cathy Brawley, Danny Allen, Leigh Torbeck, Troy Hildreth, Jessica Howard, Deanna Haskett, Tom Mangas. Ned Mitchell and I gave a speech in the barn and thanked everyone for coming. More people lay down next to Jeff and went to sleep or passed out, one by one. It became a sleepover. Becky Scheele was there with her camera taking pictures of it all.

Sometime around four-thirty a.m., Jennie, Joey, Diane, Laura, Hether, and I went upstairs to Jennie's room and curled up on the floor or the bed or the chair, wherever we could find a place. Hill was already there, sleeping off the pot. One by one we dropped off—Joey and I lasted the longest.

"We've graduated," he said. His voice sounded far away in the dark.

"Finally," I said.

"I'm drunk," he said.

"And young," I said.

"And twenty," he said.

"And could never die."

We drifted off into sleep. It was our first day as adults and we were very tired.

(On the Way to)
The Real World

Like seniors down through the years, we face the
future with a feeling of uncertainty. Though we were
big shots this year, we are now preparing to face
a freshman year as greenies in college, a period
of being a novice in some job, or even time to be
spent struggling to find work or start a family. Many
of us have grown up together, physically, emotionally,
socially, and intellectually, and now we separate to go
our individual ways. The question on just about every
senior's mind, whether he wants to admit it or not, is: "*Is
there life after high school?*"

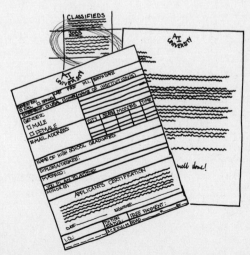

Joey and Jennifer

The Last Party

I had a dream that you looked up Tom Dehner and he was as big as a house, and you married Teresa, and I lost all the hair on the top of my head (if you can believe I, Queen Big Hair, could ever go bald). Well, best friend I've ever had, it's hard to believe it all started in a geometry class taught by a man named Bernie Foos. We've had the best friendship of anyone I know and have ever known. I have a good feeling that we'll always be best friends, no matter how far away from Richmond we get.

—*Jennifer to Joey, on the last day of senior year*

Seven days after graduation, my mother and I moved to North Carolina. To my friends, who knew nothing of my parents' separation, it was just one more summer trip to the South for me and my family, my dad staying behind as he often did, to keep working at Earlham. From North Carolina, I wrote them letters to tell them what had happened.

But in August I came back to Richmond for the last party before college, and stayed with my dad in our old house, which now had a for-sale sign in the front yard. Dean Waldemar hosted the party way out in the country in New Paris, Ohio, on a farm with a pond for swimming and a barn for dancing. It was one of those nights when everyone was there—not just the cool kids, but the hoods and the geeks and the normal kids and Tommy Wissel, who seemed to fit in wherever he damn well pleased, and us. The barriers were down, for just a night, and we weren't categories or labels but what we were: a bunch of kids from the same big school in the same small town. For some of us, we'd already reached our peak, and for the rest of us, everything was just beginning.

Joey and Laura and I each wrote about the party afterward, exchanging our versions with one another, because what happened there felt pivotal and important in some way, and we felt a strange sense of urgency to capture it all on paper so that we would always be able to remember.

Upon Remembering and Saying Farewell
August 6, 1986

By Jennifer McJunkin

The Beginning of an Evening

There is music coming from the barn and the sound of laughter and yelling as people spill out under the broad Indiana sky. The exact same songs that have played at every high school party I've ever been to are playing now.

Laura and I walk carefully because the ground is uneven and the moon keeps disappearing through the trees. Laura is chain-smoking and drinking Peach Schnapps. Every time she loses her footing, she swears in Italian. Sheila Loeber walks by and hugs me and then hugs her and Laura drops her cigarette. She swears again and squats down to look for it. I get down on my knees in my red and white sundress, helping Laura in her search.

Tom Mangas appears. "Hey, Tom," I shout, but he tells me he is upset and would rather talk later.

The first people we see are Roger Tye and Danny Dickman and Travis Cummins, with his hair cut short. Travis keeps saying things like, "I'm a trained killer. The Marines put me through this program and taught me how."

I stand there, grinning stupidly, wondering what I'm supposed to say to something like this, and finally end up saying, "Really? I wondered what you'd been up to!"

The Evening Is Full of (Blond) Men

Roger Tye is standing a few feet away with a very platinum Alex Delaney, and I haven't seen him in a long time, ever since he left for college the summer before my senior year. I choose an opportune moment when Alex is bending down doing something so Roger sees me first.

"Roger," I say, waving my vodka bottle. "I've been in North Carolina for two months, and you haven't written me once."

Before he can answer, Alex has stood up and grabbed my arm and is staring openmouthed. He smiles and we hug. "Jen!" (I had wondered what it was he used to call me.) "You look *wonderful*!" His forehead creases in concern. "But I heard about your parents. How are you really?"

I laugh and don't answer and tell him I like his hair. He calls me "Gorgeous," and I change my mind and remember that this was what he had called me when we were together. John Dehner is somewhere around and it is his car I lean upon. Alex tells me so and I remember narrowly the time he and I went shopping at Loehr's and John gave me a Coke and I was so thrilled I couldn't finish it.

Alex and I can't talk fast enough and Danny Dickman is back and I am leaning on his shoulder. His arm is around my waist and Alex is staring at it. Someone—Roger, I think—tells me Jennie and Hill have arrived and I can't understand him and he points and there they are, so I run and hug (1) Jennie and (2) Hill. I am happy to see them because they are smiling and my friends and I have only five girlfriends anyway, and that isn't much. They want to know if I'm okay, what with my parents splitting up, they had no idea, why hadn't I told them what was going on, how was I handling it, etc., and I am so sick of people talking to me about this and wanting to know how I'm doing.

Ronnie Stier, Larry Peterson, and Ned Mitchell, wearing a Reebok shirt, sit at a picnic table watching Ricky Grimes and Tommy Wissel roll joints. When "Tom Sawyer" by Rush comes on, Ned Mitchell says, as always, "Neil Peart is the best drummer in music today." No one ever argues with him, but he always feels the need to say it.

Joey appears, begs Ricky for a cigarette, gets one, pledges his eternal gratitude, and proceeds to puff away in Cliff Lester's face. Cliff wants to know again why I went to junior year Homecoming with Curt Atkisson instead of him. He begins to lecture Joey, and Joey begins to smoke two cigarettes at once so that Cliff will leave. As soon as he does, Joey scoots down to talk to Ronnie, Larry, and Ned, who are talking about college and virginity. Ronnie crushes a Coors can against his forehead.

Ross walks by—a great, hulking shadow in the distance—and yells at Joey: "You nearly killed yourself driving like that last night, asshole." Joey blows smoke in his direction.

Deanna Haskett and Tamela Vance are talking. "I don't want to be some housewife or something when I grow up," Deanna says. "Me neither," says Tamela. "If I do, I will kill myself."

Rip appears and Joey tells her he wants his red tie back, the one he lost at her house after Snowball. She calls him an alcoholic and announces that it is over between her and Tom Dehner. "Where is he?" I ask, and then someone

points and there he is in the distance surrounded by Sean
Mayberry and the other black football players, the ones
who always swarm around him like those fish that stick to
a shark.

Suddenly someone appears out of the dark. He is with
one of those old men who is always hanging around—one of
those guys who graduated from RHS five or ten years ago but
still comes to parties. It takes a minute, but suddenly it hits
me: Dean Waldemar. He is a god. Especially now. College
has even improved him. His hair is very blond and damp
and tousled and he wears a sweatshirt and shorts. He still has
that lean swimmer's body—broad shoulders, narrow waist,
flat stomach, tan legs with little gold hairs up and down the
calves. And his eyes are large and beautiful and dark and
bloodshot and his smile is wonderfully crooked as he says,
"Jennifer."

There is a twist in my stomach as I think about all that
might have been between us, if Tim Bullen hadn't spread lies
and rumors just because I'd turned him down, and if Dean
hadn't listened, and if he had asked me out like I heard he
always wanted to. He would have been my first real love,
I knew. He would have been worth any amount of heartbreak. We would probably have still been together.

I say, "Dean Waldemar, do you know I came nine hours
to go to your party?"

He whispers in my ear, "I'm coming back for you in a
minute."

He is momentarily gone, and I return to the ever-
growing group around John Dehner's car. Alex is watching
me, studying my face. I love everyone and suddenly need
to lean against something or sit down—not from alcohol,
but from Dean. Danny helps me onto the hood of John's

car. I lean my hand on Danny's shoulder because my dress is slippery and I keep sliding off. He is so sturdy and nice, such a good, steady friend, and Alex wants to know again when I got here, and how I am really, and I keep smiling, taking a sip of Danny's beer, and tell Alex how much I really like his hair.

The End of an Evening

When Phil Collins's "In the Air Tonight" starts, we all sing along. It is this song, more than any other, that makes me think of RHS, of corn and barns and moonlight and wide open skies. We all climb up on the tops of picnic tables and dance, and when the drums kick in, every single person holds air drumsticks and plays along.

Sometime much later, Joey and I are standing alone waiting for Laura when we see Tom Dehner, without his baseball hat, coming straight for us. He is wearing a blue DePauw sweatshirt and he is alone, which is strange because never in our lives have we known him to be by himself.

"Have you seen Rip?" he says to us.

"She was looking for you earlier," Joey says, "but I think it's too late. I think she left."

"I hope not," he says, then hesitates. He stands there and he looks uncertain, as if he doesn't know which way to go.

"Will you miss me, Tom?" I ask. I don't know why I say it. After three years, after we formed a history team for him and a speech team and wrote a play just for him, we barely know each other.

He pauses and then says, "Yes. I'll miss you very much."

Then he is gone. Joey and I stand there watching him disappear into the night—nothing more than a sincere, regular human being, after all we have built him up to be.

And the life is gone from the August 6 party.

Afterward, Joey drives Laura and me to his house, where we sit on his back deck beneath the stars—which, for once, aren't too bright or too many or too far or too close—and hold hands and cry. We don't want to leave the deck or one another. We start laughing till we can't breathe. We are best friends outside in the night on August 6 no matter what— no matter where we go, no matter what happens, no matter who we meet, no matter where life takes us.

After a long time, we leave Laura at her house, which is empty except for her, and Joey drives me home. We know that it is our last evening together for a long time to come, and there is a sorrow in that, but a richness, too. We know that there will never be a final evening to our friendship— how can there be? The air is damp, the moon is up, the tank is full, the hour is still (somewhat) young, the curfews are late, and the summer is not yet over.

We decide to drive around a bit, just for old times, before he takes me home. We pass down a backcountry road. The headlights of Joey's car—actually his mom's car—are the only speck of light for miles. Then Joey turns off all the car lights and the music and we head down a long corridor walled by corn on either side. We roll the windows down, and everything is quiet and still and dark except for the blue tint of the clock on the dashboard.

"We'll be gone soon," I say.

"And alone," he says.

We shiver, like always, and I feel suddenly separate from everything—from the party, from Joey, from my parents, from myself. In the distance, we can see the lights of Richmond.

I say, "Do you realize that we're not going back to high school in the fall, and that we won't see each other every day, and my room won't be my room anymore but someone else's?"

"Leaving home and friends and traveling many hours to a school where we don't know anyone to live with someone we know absolutely nothing about," Joey says.

We turn the headlights back on, roll up the windows, crank the music. We have gotten ourselves too spooked, too sad. We drive without talking, and when we hit the turn to National Road West, which will take me back to my old house—my dad's house now—Joey continues straight instead.

The high school appears, dark and enormous. We turn into the parking lot next to McGuire Hall and pull around back, where I used to wait at the double doors for my dad to pick me up. The lot is empty. We pop in a tape—the Talking Heads' "Road to Nowhere"—and we turn it loud.

There is a large, yellow circle on the concrete, used maybe to strengthen technique or precision in a Driver's Education class. I think about Mr. Kemper and Tom Mangas and Tommy Wissel and the simulators, and Mr. Fleagle slamming his foot against the emergency brake over and over.

As the music picks up speed, Joey and I run, arms outstretched like airplane wings, around and around in circles, following that wide yellow line. We frantically run those lines, following the perfect circles they make, music spilling from the car, yelling. We shout and laugh and sing along loudly. We are alone in that parking lot we've known for years, the grand spire of our school illuminated by spotlights high above us. I feel homesick and free all at once as we sing words that echo graduation and a longing to return to bygone places.

It is our last night to be children, and we are spectacles in the moonlight.

The Postscript

In front of my house Joey and I say good-bye, but not really good-bye, and we wonder when we will see each other again. It is all very vague and sad and anticlimactic, and then he drives away.

I go inside and my dad is asleep and I try not to think of the days when my mom would wait up for me—every single time—until I got in, just to make sure I was safe. She could never sleep until she knew I was home. I think that my dad has probably been asleep for hours.

I walk up the stairs to my room—my green room—and turn on the light. My posters are still there. My dollhouse. My records. My books. The picture of Laura and Todd Irwin and me at Devon Johnson's party is still taped to my mirror. Pictures of Joey and me. Of Prom. Of Ross and Hether and Alex and Matt Ashton. Of Jennie, Hill, Hether, Diane, Laura, Joey, and me at my birthday dinner, the night they gave me the Swatch. My yearbooks and dolls and stuffed animals and toys.

I sit there feeling sad and lonely and the house is very quiet and I am leaving the next day and college is starting soon and I wonder what the world holds and if I'm ready for it and how my dad can really sleep through it all.

And then I hear something hit my window.

I go to the window and raise the blind—the one with the funny zoo animals in bright colors that I never replaced even though I sometimes hated them and long-ago outgrew them. Even as I'm peering out into the night, I wonder vaguely what my dad will do with the blinds once I'm gone again, this time really and truly for good.

Alex Delaney is standing on my front porch step, his hair shining white in the porch light. He is throwing pebbles at my window.

I turn off my bedroom light and sneak down the hall and run down the stairs, hoping Tosh won't bark, and slip out the door. Alex and I hug for a long, long time, and he is sexy and warm and we fall into each other and kiss and kiss and kiss and kiss and it's just like he never left and I never broke up with him and my parents never separated and I never moved, and I wonder if I hold on to him long enough if I can go back in time, back to when we were together and he would walk me to class and write me notes and pick me up in his red car and even back to when he bought me the bear. Back to when my mom still lived here and I still lived here and everything was happy and in its place. And then I shiver and we sit side by side on the step.

"Why are you here?" I ask.

"I'm staying with Travis." Travis Cummins lives around the corner from my old house.

"He's in the military now," I say because suddenly I don't know what to say and I'm afraid of what comes next. "His hair is so short!"

"I know." Alex drops the pebbles into the grass and looks at me. "So how are you really?"

It is just like when we used to date, when Alex would try to get to know me. "You're like this series of boxes," he would say, "and every time I open one box, there's another one inside, and then there's one inside that, and then another, and just when I think I'm getting somewhere, there's another and another." I never told him that I don't open the boxes for just anyone, not for most people, and that so far there has really only been one boy allowed to look in them, and I just said good-bye to him minutes ago.

"I'm worried about you," Alex says. His voice is small. He looks hurt and lost. "You've got so much going on. How are you really?"

I want to say that he doesn't need to worry, that everything is fine now because he is here and I'm pretending nothing has changed—my parents' separation never happened, Tim Bullen never happened. Everything is fine. Dean Waldemar has finally told me what I always wanted to hear and it is just a little something, but a big thing, too. *I'm sorry,* Dean said when he found me again at the party. *I'm sorry I was so stupid in high school. I wish I'd asked you out. I should have asked you out. I wanted to, but I was too shy and then there was all that stuff with Tim, and I let it get in the way even though I knew he was a liar.*

I want to say to Alex that, in the end, Tim Bullen hadn't won with the rumors he spread and the lies he told because Dean and I had still found each other, even if it was just for a moment at a party in the middle of nowhere, and that it had been a wonderful moment in the midst of too much darkness—brief and bright and lovely.

But that would be opening too many boxes. And besides, everything isn't fine. Everything is far from it. Because it isn't 1985, and my mother isn't inside, and Alex and I aren't together, and I don't live here anymore. There are so many things to say.

Instead, I rest my head on Alex's shoulder, and he smells

like he always did—of laundry detergent and Clearasil and, faintly, of cigarettes and beer—and I close my eyes and we sit there. "I'm tired," I say. "But I'm glad you're here."

And then he kisses me again. And I kiss him. And he kisses me. And then he takes my hand and holds it.

RICHMOND HIGH SCHOOL
Class of 1986

Alumni

With each name comes a story. But all stories have a common chapter of high school. Those years form our lives. Unlike college or careers, high school touches our hearts in a different way. It opens the door more slowly—allowing us to invest ourselves in other people in a manner that we just don't take the time for later in life.

Jennifer then and now

Jennifer Niven

Jennifer Niven lives in Los Angeles, where her film *Velva Jean Learns to Drive* won an Emmy Award and she received her MFA in screenwriting from the American Film Institute. She is also a graduate of Drew University in Madison, New Jersey. Even though she's always wanted to be a rock star and a Charlie's Angel, her first book, *The Ice Master*, was released in November 2000 and named one of the Top Ten Nonfiction Books of the Year by *Entertainment Weekly*. A Barnes & Noble Discover Great New Writer, Jennifer has ten different publishers in ten separate countries, and the book has been translated into German, French, Italian, Portuguese, Chinese, Danish, and Icelandic, among other languages.

Jennifer and *The Ice Master* have appeared in *Newsweek*, *Entertainment Weekly*, *Glamour*, *The New Yorker*, *Outside*, *The New York Times Book Review*, *The London Daily Mail*, and *Writer's Digest*, among others. *Dateline NBC*, the *Discovery Channel*, and the *History Channel* have featured *The Ice Master* in hour-long documentaries, and *The Ice Master* has been nominated for awards by the American Library Association and Book Sense, and received Italy's Gambrinus Giuseppe Mazzotti Prize for 2002.

Jennifer's second book, *Ada Blackjack*, was released in November 2003. It was a Book Sense Top Ten Pick, was optioned for the movies, has recently been published in China, and will soon be released in France and Estonia.

Jennifer's third book and first novel, *Velva Jean Learns to Drive*—based on her Emmy Award–winning film of the same name—was released by Plume in 2009.

With her mother, author Penelope Niven, Jennifer has conducted numerous seminars in writing and she has addressed audiences around the world. Although she no longer wears Esprit, she still loves pretty clothes, tambourines, ABBA, hair spray, rock stars, and continues to be fascinated by prisons.

Joey then and now

Joe Kraemer

Joe Kraemer is the Drama Division's literary director at the Juilliard School in New York City. He oversees a fellowship program for playwrights and has helped to discover many talented young writers from around the United States and the world. He created the program with John Guare and Terrence McNally and has worked since 1994 with the program's current mentors, Christopher Durang and Marsha Norman.

His plays *Find Some Planets*, *The American Occupation*, and *Dangerous People* were created for actors at Juilliard and performed at the school.

Joe is also director of creative development for Estevez Sheen Productions at Warner Bros. in Los Angeles. While he has had several lunches with Emilio Estevez, he has yet to mention the impact *St. Elmo's Fire* once had on his life.

Joe received his BA in English from Hillsdale College in Michigan. For the past three years, he has taught playwriting at Barnard College in New York, where he currently lives, and where he drives as little as possible.

Laura Lonigro

Laura earned her BFA at Indiana University, with a major in English and a minor in theater. After college, she attended graduate school at Columbia College in Chicago, studying film and video. She has worked on numerous short films as both a writer and director, and has also worked on national spots—commercials, industrials, and feature films. Performance-wise, she has continued training in improv, film, and theater productions, mostly at the Piven Theater (owned and operated by Jeremy Piven's parents).

She continues to write and direct today. Her last movie, *Brushfires,* was filmed, written, and directed by seven different women using the same style of writing so loved by our little group back in Richmond—writing one chapter at a time and handing it off to the next woman to see how she continues the story.

Laura still lives in Chicago, Illinois, with her enormous handbag, killer heels, and gallons of hair spray, and continues to work on a variety of film and video projects.

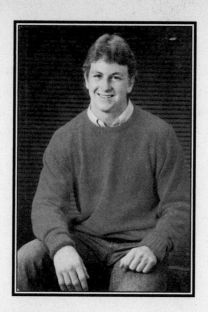

Tom Dehner

Tom Dehner is Medicaid director in the Executive Office of Health and Human Services (EOHHS) of the Commonwealth of Massachusetts. Tom provides strategic policy direction, directs clinical policy, negotiates with federal and state regulators, and supervises plan operations for a health insurance program that covers more than one million members.

Tom came to MassHealth in 2003 as chief of staff of the Division of Medical Assistance. In February 2004, Tom was named deputy Medicaid director. Before coming to work at MassHealth, Tom earned his law degree from Northeastern University. He later served as counsel to the Massachusetts Senate Committee on Ways and Means, where he supervised legislative policy on insurance matters and health care.

He is married and has three children. About his days at Richmond High School, he says, "Unless I was mistaken, Tom Mangas was the golden king of RHS. To me, he still is. I was just a lucky kid."

Teresa (Ripperger) Radtke

As Teresa says, "Richmond High School was a great experience." After high school Teresa attended Indiana University (Bloomington), where her relationship with Tom Dehner ended. Tom attended DePauw University and began dating someone almost immediately. "In retrospect, it was the biggest heartbreak of my life," Teresa says, "but it was inevitable. We remained friends, though. I will always have a warm place in my heart for my first love."

Teresa met Tim Radtke at IU, they dated for six years, and they were married in 1992. They have two sons, Jake and Luke. They live in Muncie, Indiana, and chose to raise the boys in a smaller community very similar to Richmond. Tim's high school experience was at a Catholic high school in Chicago, so Teresa had to convince him that a smaller public high school in Indiana was a good thing. Once Tim met friends and family from Richmond he agreed.

Teresa has a successful sales career and continues to balance her career and motherhood. She says Tim is her rock and keeps her focused. She is just as social as she was in her high school days. She owes her leadership skills, confidence, and passion to RHS.

Eric Lundquist

Eric Lundquist lives in Chicago, where he is a process development scientist for Abbott Laboratories. ("Basically, if you see on the news someone manipulating red liquid in a Petri dish, that's what I do—but on a large scale.") He's happily married and has two beautiful daughters.

He said his parents live in the same house in Richmond, the one he grew up in. Over the years, his mom has clipped out articles from the *Palladium-Item* relating to my books and to my father's death and sent them to Eric. He told me he's proud of me. I told him how much he meant to me and how sorry I was for the way I acted when I was silly and sixteen. He said the smiley face I drew, all those years ago, is still there on the basement chalkboard.

Alex Delaney

After high school, Alex traveled the country in a van, following the Grateful Dead from state to state, city to city. He belonged to a hippie cartel, living a carefree lifestyle, part of the counterculture. Now he lives in Colorado. He is, according to him, one part Grizzly Adams, one part Buddhist monk. He has never married and is an accomplished stonemason, one of the best known, most in-demand in the state. His brother Chris was killed nine years ago in a kayaking accident and Alex says that tragic loss opened the world to him. He now makes the most of every day, traveling the world when he can, scuba diving, snowboarding, snorkeling with whale sharks.

When we spoke recently, he told me about his dog Vela, who was just a puppy when he inherited her from Chris. He said, "I guess you could say she's the third most significant woman in my life. The first two were Diane Weigle and you."

I said, "Can I put that in the book?"

He said, "You can put it all in, sweetheart. I'm just honored to be included."

Tommy Wissel

In 1989, Tommy joined the navy at the start of the Persian Gulf War. As he says, he saw a lot of the world as well as a lot of devastation. "It really makes you appreciate what we have." He married Pam, the girl from County Market, that same year. He got out of the navy in 1993 and moved back to Indiana, where he worked for Dana Corporation. In 2004 Dana moved its operations to Mexico, and, Tommy says, "with the grades I got in Spanish (and the fact that I once pissed off Señor Sackett so bad that he sent himself to the office), I figured this probably was not a good transition for me." So he took advantage of the tuition-free schooling offered for displaced workers and received a degree in electronics. He is now the maintenance supervisor at Smith Dairy in Richmond. He and Pam and their five kids—Maggie, Emily, Jacob, Katie, and Sarah—live in Lynn, Indiana, and his children attend Randolph Southern schools (one in every even grade except sixth). Tommy and Pam will celebrate their twentieth wedding anniversary this year.

Whenever things get a little too intense around the house—whenever the girls overrun things—Tommy says to his son, "Jake, let's go get some ice cream." That's their code to get out and take a break. Mostly he tries to keep his kids from pulling anything over on him or running too wild like he used to. He says they're surprisingly—shockingly—well behaved.

Tom Mangas, Heather Craig, Dan Allen, Jennifer Niven, Teresa Ripperger, Sherri Dillon, and Tommy Wissel

Extra Credit

It's got a tiny skyscape,
And the people are happy here . . .
Back again in Richmond,
Where the people all drive slow,
Back again in Richmond,
Where the people never go!

—*"Back Again in Richmond," original song by Jennifer and Joey*

Each book is a journey. The journey of my first two books was rewarding and very special. The third, my novel, was deeply fulfilling in ways I can't describe. But the journey of writing this book was by far the most laugh-out-loud, tease-your-hair-up fun. It was also surprisingly moving. It took me back to a happy time when my dad was alive and my parents were together, when Joey lived just across town, when I was young and silly and hadn't ever lost anything or anyone, and it reunited me with some wonderful people. It also made me feel unnervingly like a high school girl again.

The research was very different this time around. Instead of archives and libraries, I talked to real people and dug through my own memories. Mary Lou Griffey, alumni director at Richmond High School, generously gave me access to numerous yearbook photos spanning nearly a hundred years. After sorting through thousands of pictures, I stumbled across a photo of Joey, Laura, and myself from our *Judy on Purpose* photo shoot. The file was titled "High Hair," and Mary said it had been used in a display at the school as *the* single example of 1980s hairstyles. "Great," said Laura when I told her about it. "Of all the hair in all the years of that entire decade, they of course chose us."

The thing about writing a memoir is that if you want to use people's real names it can be a good idea to get their okay to use those names in your book. This is something that didn't occur to me when I sold my book about high school. At the time I sent out the proposal, I was having so much fun reliving every silly, embarrassing, humiliating, crazy adventure I had back in Richmond, that I didn't stop to think about the other people involved in those adventures. The ones I would decide to contact to say:

Dear So-and-So,

I know we haven't seen each other in twenty years. I hope you're doing well. I'm writing a book about our high school years at Richmond High School (I know-right? Someone is actually paying me to write this!), and remember the time we (insert insane, incriminating incident here)? Well, I would just love your okay to use your real name and publish it in a book for all your friends and family and neighbors and co-workers to see. Also, remember our big hair and bad 80s fashions? I want to include pictures, too, so while you're at it, I'd love to get your okay to use some really funny and embarrassing photos from back then. Thanks! Hope life is great otherwise!

All my best,
Jennifer

You can imagine how much fun it was to contact my classmates. And what the response was like, especially since they are all mothers and fathers and hard workers and businesspeople and heads of companies and upstanding, responsible citizens now.

Some of my favorite replies:

From Tom Mangas: "I'll be happy to help in any way I can. Just as long as you change my name."

From Jeff Shirazi: "Um. What exactly is going to be in this book? Just how risqué are you planning to get?"

From one of the cheerleaders (re. the subject of making out): "Jennifer, do not put this in the book! I don't want my children to think their mother was a slut!"

From Curt Atkisson: "Turned 40 yet? That dread can only be matched by finding out that a woman you dated in high school who became a well-known writer is now writing an autobiographical book."

From my own mother: "I've just decided that I would like you to change my name in this book."

Is it any wonder that, when I proposed an in-person minireunion for the purpose of sharing stories and pictures and memories, it was almost impossible to (a) choose a date, and (b) get people together? Remember that I did not go to a small school.

No, RHS is huge and our class was huge, which means there were many, many people to contact before this book could ever see the light of day. But the minireunion (in Richmond, of course) was fun and everyone was amazingly supportive. Jeff Shirazi even rented a plane and flew it himself from Columbus, Ohio, to the Richmond Municipal Airport so he could bring me some albums of high school pictures. (Which made my high school self squeal: *Oh my God! Jeff Shirazi is renting a plane to come meet me!*)

At the minireunion, we relived the old stories. We laughed so hard my stomach hurt for days afterward. My classmates let me photograph them. They let me record them as we talked and laughed and talked and laughed. They shared stories with me that I had never heard. They agreed to let me use their names in the book. Even Tom Mangas changed his mind and agreed (albeit tentatively, warily), although he had visited with his mother before coming to meet us and received the following advice: "Be careful what you say because she might write it down!"

They have given me their full support, these former classmates of mine. Everyone has been great (far better than I would have been given the subject matter!), but I do have to single out a few folks:

Joe Kraemer, without whom none of these pages would exist. I wouldn't have survived Richmond (college, Los Angeles, *life*) without him. Thanks for being, bar none, my BFF.

Eloise Larkin Abernathy (the pseudonym my mother, Penelope Niven, suggested I use to conceal her identity in this book) who taught me all about Big Dreams and who has learned many a shocking thing about her daughter while reading this manuscript, but who continues to love me anyway.

Jack F. McJunkin Jr., fastest father on earth (be it in car or on foot), who isn't here to see this book, but who lived through much of it while it was happening with great patience, style, and humor (I realize now in retrospect).

John Hreno, who has been to every reunion and who knows every story.

Laura Lonigro—best girlfriend ever. Thanks for pictures, late-night phone calls, laughter, memories, and moving to Richmond all those years ago. What on earth would I have done without her?

Heather Craig, for being there before anyone else, and for being there again.

Teresa Ripperger Radtke, for her enthusiasm, generous help, and for nearly out–Harper Leeing Joey. If you are writing a book and need something organized, call Teresa!

Jeff Shirazi, for going the extra air miles and for entrusting me with his photo albums.

Tommy Wissel, for some of the funniest (and most unprintable) stories I've ever heard. He is a book all by himself.

Eric Lundquist, for first love.

Alex Delaney, for the bear, for boxes opened, and for himself.

Dan and Kim Allen, for going above and beyond.

Tom Dehner, for his generous, modest self. I giggled for five full minutes after talking to him on the phone the first time, and, of course, called Joey immediately afterward to tell him all about it. (*"Oh my God! I just talked to Tom Dehner!"*)

Shane M., for Barrett Attic days, *Sounds from the Attic*, and letting this high school girl hang out with him.

Tom Mangas, for letting me use his real name.

Sherri Dillon Bergum, for proving me wrong about cheerleaders, and for sharing her newfound sparkling wit.

Becky Scheele, for party pictures, yearbooks, girl time, and for "keeping it real."

Hether Rielly Schlosser (fastest driver in the Midwest), Curtis Atkisson, Ross Vigran, Lisa Fanning, Dan Mikeska, Robert Ignacio, Ronnie Stier, Leigh Torbeck Walkotte, Todd Irwin, and Troy Hildreth for all their help.

Mr. Van Shank, for saving me from *Flossy Flamingo* and showing me what a great teacher truly is.

Mary Lou Griffey, Rachel Sheeley, and Sue King—three marvelous researchers and treasured friends.

Mike and Melanie Kraemer, my adopted parents, who rescued Joey and me from more than one catastrophe with the car, and who have miraculously managed to maintain their sense of humor and their youthful good looks.

Penelope Niven, John Hreno, Roy Hall, Angelo Surmelis, and Lisa Brucker, who didn't go to high school with me but who read the book in its rough form and got it. I crown you honorary kings and queens!

John Ware, my remarkable agent and friend, for his constant encouragement and his faith in this project. He would have made a terrific cheerleader (in the best sense of the word!).

The amazing team at Simon Spotlight—Jennifer Bergstrom and Tricia Boczkowski, Katie Rizzo, and Michael Nagin for the super-cool cover. And most of all to Sarah Sper, kindred spirit as well as dynamite editor supreme.

Charlie Sheen, Ramon Estevez, and David Woodbury for believing in this book, and Lisa Lang, Wendy Steinhoff, and everybody at Warner Bros. for seeing its small-screen potential.

Satchmo, Rumi, and Lulu, the most involved, devoted literary cats I've ever known.

Heather Webb, for making my hair much smaller than it was in high school.

And to Richmond High School, Dennis Middle School, Westview Elementary School, Earlham College, Morrisson-Reeves Library, the *Palladium-Item*, the Wayne County Vistor's Center, and, most of all, to Richmond, Indiana, my hometown. I hope you'll still let me visit after you read this book.

Q & A *with Jennifer Niven McJunkin*

- *Who were you in high school?* I was sometimes a brain, sometimes a beauty, sometimes a rebel, sometimes the girl next door, sometimes popular, sometimes a wallflower, sometimes Scarlett O'Hara at the barbecue. I was a chameleon.
- *Who did you want to be in high school?* Demi Moore, Scarlett O'Hara, Jaclyn Smith, George Sand, Stevie Nicks, Frida from ABBA, Jane Austen, Belinda Carlisle, Debbie Harry. I wanted to be anyone larger than life who moved on the world stage.
- *Who are you now (in what ways are you similar to your high school self)?* I'm still more comfortable with men than with women and I still trust men more (other than my mother, the women in my family, and a handful of girlfriends). I'm still a flirt. I still feel like an outsider some-

times, especially in smaller places. I'm confident and I know who I am. I'm an artist. I'm boy crazy. I'm silly. I'm disciplined. I'm serious. I'm spontaneous. I want everyone to like me. I try to please people. I'm happy. I have fun all the time. I worry about everything. I'm positive. I am younger than my age. I dream big. I think anything is possible. I still plan to be a rock star. I am constantly growing at lightning speed. I like loud music and driving fast. None of these things have changed.

- *If you had to label your high school self in a simple category, what would that be?* On a more superficial level, I was the flirt. On a deeper level, I was the outsider. I never truly felt like I fit in, although I wanted to.

- *What do you think made your high school experience so unique/special?* There was something about that one enormous high school in that one small town. All eyes were on us. We were all collected into one school. Even when I was dying to get out of Richmond and RHS and go far, far away to the big city, there was still a part of me that was proud of that big, grand high school and the impression it made, the pride the town took in it, the quirky and charming town itself, and the colorful characters unique to Richmond. I remember the way my classmates looked at me when I went to college in New Jersey—with people who'd grown up in Manhattan or Philadelphia or Boston or L.A. When I said I grew up in Indiana, they looked at me as if I was from Mars. And there was a part of me that really enjoyed that.

- *What's the most valuable thing you learned from your high school experience?* Besides learning to type, I learned to talk about things that affect you, even if someone says you shouldn't. Not to hold things in because this can damage you—it's not healthy. To let people see inside those boxes. To really experience what's in front of you at the moment without always looking ahead toward the next thing, because you just might miss what's right there. And what was right there in front of me were some pretty incredible people in a pretty incredible place. I'm glad I was able to realize it before I left.

For the Reader . . .

Now it's your turn . . .

High School Questions

- Who were you in high school?
- Who did you want to be in high school?
- Who are you now (in what ways are you similar to your high school self)?
- If you had to label your high school self in a simple category, what would that be? (Were you the jock, the brain, the nerd, the geek, the wallflower, etc.?)
- What do you think made your high school experience so unique/special?
- Craziest memories?

- Funniest memories?
- Hardest/saddest memories?
- Can you share specific memories of the following:
  - Teachers (Those you hated, those you loved; funniest, favorite, most memorable classroom moments.)
  - Skipping school
  - Detention/other punishments (Specific times you might have gotten into trouble.)
  - Breakups (Friendships? Romances?)
  - Sex and dating (Did you feel like everyone was doing it but you? Were you doing it? Did you want to do it but had no one to do it with? Did you do it but wish you'd waited?)
  - Parties (Do any specific party moments stand out? Funny ones? Scary ones?)
  - Anything else you want to add?
- What's the most valuable thing you learned from your high school experience?